NEW VOICES IN AMERICAN POETRY: AN ANTHOLOGY

Edited by

DAVID ALLAN EVANS

South Dakota State University
Brookings, South Dakota

WINTHROP PUBLISHERS, INC.

CAMBRIDGE, MASSACHUSETTS

Library of Congress Cataloging in Publication Data

Evans, David Allan, comp.
    New voices in American poetry: an anthology.

    1. American poetry—20th century.   I. Title.
PS613.E9   811'.5'408   72–12943
ISBN 0–87626–613–8

cover and design by Joe Guertin

Copyright © 1973 by Winthrop Publishers, Inc.
17 Dunster Street, Cambridge, Massachusetts 02138

for Jan, my wife

Preface

New Voices In American Poetry is an anthology of poems and essays by forty-five new American poets. The combination of poetry and critiques by the poets is, I believe, especially appropriate for courses in creative writing—where such things as technique and style are observed at close range—as well as for courses in contemporary poetry. The book is not, however, intended exclusively as a textbook. I like to think it will be read by anyone interested in what E. A. Robinson called "the possible conjunction of a few inevitable words," and by anyone interested in contemporary American life.

The decision to include comments by the poets on their poems rests on the assumption that what writers say about their work, and how they say it, are both interesting and instructive for anyone who is curious about the process of the creative mind. I also believe that an essay on a specific poem is more valuable to the reader (and probably to the writer) than, say, something called "Why I Write Poems."

This anthology is certainly not intended as a definitive selection of poems by new or young American poets. There are simply too many good, new poets for any "definitive" selection to be possible. I, therefore, regret the omission of many poets whose work deserves wide recognition, and sincerely hope that it will find the recognition it deserves elsewhere.

I want to thank Philip Dacey and Raymond Carver for their assistance, and Donald Justice, poet and professor of English at the University of Iowa, for his Introduction.

DAVID ALLAN EVANS

Contents

Contents vii

Introduction

Ideas, I sometimes think, are in the saddle and ride our poetry: notions of classification, dreams of the future. But these were from the start the inventions of critics, making their job possible, or of poets turned aside from their own best nature by weak self-love or strong self-hatred, turned for a time into just such critics, preachers to the not quite saved, leaders of armies. To serve another's convenience we have been divided if not in the end conquered. How satisfying it must always be to the critic in each of us to be able to identify what will pass at the moment as instant virtue: a certain disposition of the lines on a page, some illusion of substance in the guise of cause or attitude, perhaps no more than the repetition of a slogan or code-word, signifying allegiance. I have a nightmare vision filled with chimeric figures, faces I half recognize and could almost put names to, voices that shout, arms that wave for attention. And, after all, they are only editors and critics, spokesmen or showmen who because they know where our poetry is and where it should be heading must therefore lead us somewhere or other. In their missionary fervor all these St. Pauls of poetry, because they do care so much (perhaps) would leave us behind if we show ourselves unready to follow them into or out of their version of wilderness.

Anthologists often enough have succumbed to this critical passion. The result has been a number of collections which, representing a school or a style, would point a direction for the poetry of the future. Now this is an instructive function for an anthology to serve—classification, definition, illustration; but for pleasure, and a pleasure which can carry with it its own kind of instruction, I still prefer a sort of Tottel's Miscellany approach. It is the latter type of anthology we have here, insofar as it is eclectic and ranging, using only age and place—young poets in America—as preliminary grounds for choice. The poets and their poems do not seem to be here because their work defines a movement or even because it represents in its diversity styles now in fashion. Instead I understand the selections to be the editor's judgment, according to his own lights, of what was among the best work available to him of the many excellent young writers there are. What those lights may be the poems themselves will best declare, but I think I can say at least that the aesthetic grounds seem not to have been fixed and predetermined but shifting and flexible; and if the resulting judgment is not quite my own, or the reader's, that is properly beside the point. It is what we would have to say of any such anthology if we had not made it, and even perhaps if we had.

None of which is to deny that some of the conditions under which American poetry now suffers and thrives are amply present. Here is, for instance, that poetry of image by means of which so many poets, young and older, now join their world of rich fantasy to the real (and really absurd) world of experience. Accompanying this is the hardly to be avoided violence, violence of act and of language which is also act, that may or may not reflect the violence in our lives nowadays. Technically, the verse is what used to be called free, more or less, free to find its own rhythms and shapes as it goes: standard practice, of course, but natural here and hardly programmatic. All of this *is* representative, even—or almost—inevitable. There is, I believe, at least one great poem here (the reader will have to find it for himself), and no doubt thirty or so other terrific ones. The poets range from one or two famous enough to have been mentioned already by Robert Bly (not always favorably), some who have been around long enough to have been in Paul Carroll's first anthology, *The Young American Poets*, quite a few with a book or books out, all the way to those completely unknown—at least to me—before I encountered them here. Thus I got the pleasure I want of any good anthology, the pleasure of discovering poems and poets I did not know and might otherwise only with difficulty and luck have come across.

For novelty we have from most of the poets brief essays, not theoretical but practical, on how they came to write one or more of the poems included. Factual in most cases, sometimes mildly technical, almost all becomingly modest, and very few containing propaganda or slogans, they seem more honest than such glimpses into the workshop generally are. They speak handsomely of the intuition trusted by so many of the poets here as almost to make that, at least, one article of common faith; and go on to mention, sometimes with joy, the hard work that is part of writing poems. These essays show the way poets think when they think about poems, the way poems have been in their lives; and, incidentally, it is not often the way a critic talks about poems to us. The poets have not, for the most part, labeled themselves, and I would not try to do that either, even if I could, except to say that they are the young. They are, in truth, the young who, seen here as overwhelming us, are in reality coming to our rescue.

Our poetry is either still divided into camps, or it is all one country. Although two or three of the city-states starred on other maps of the current scene happen to be missing from this one, perhaps regrettably, I think that this anthology comes down strongly on the one-country side of the argument, if it is an argument, if it is a side. Good.

—DONALD JUSTICE

July 4, 1972

Acknowledgments

JAMES APPLEWHITE. "My Grandfather's Funeral," copyright 1966 by *Shenandoah*, reprinted by permission from *Shenandoah:* The Washington and Lee University Review, with the permission of the Editor. "Versions of Sunlight," from *Granite* (Spring, 1971), reprinted by permission. "War Summer," first printed in the *American Review;* copyright 1972 by James Applewhite. "Dream of Ascent," from *Sou'wester* (Fall, 1968), reprinted by permission.

COLEMAN BARKS. "Downy Hair in the Shape of a Flame Moving Up the Stomach and Ending at the Solar Plexis," "White Crescents at the Bottom of Fingernails and Toenails," "Semen," from *The Juice* by Coleman Barks. Copyright © 1968 by Coleman Barks. Reprinted by permission of Harper & Row, Publishers, Inc. "Achilles Tendon," "Genitals," "Cheek," "Back Just Below the Shoulder Blades," "Skeleton," "Dimple," "Liver," "Bruises," "Hair on the Chest," from *The Juice* by Coleman Barks, copyright © 1972 by Coleman Barks. Reprinted by permission of Harper & Row, Publishers, Inc. "Skull," "Scar," "Brain," from *Quickly Aging Here: Some Poets of the 1970's,* ed. by Geof Hewitt, © 1960 by Doubleday, Inc. Reprinted by permission.

MARVIN BELL. "In The Home," "American Poet," "Song: The Organic Years," from *Escape Into You* by Marvin Bell. Copyright © 1969, 1970, 1971 by Marvin Bell. Reprinted by permission of Atheneum Publishers, Inc. "In The Home," originally appeared in *Poetry*, "Song" appeared originally in *The New Yorker*. "Her Dream House," "The Delicate Bird . . . " from *A Probable Volume of Dreams* by Marvin Bell. Copyright © 1964, 1966, 1969 by Marvin Bell. Reprinted by permission of Atheneum Publishers, Inc. "Her Dream House" originally appeared in *Poetry*.

HAROLD BOND. "It Is Oregon: The Highway Looms," "Girls Who Wave At Cars From Bridges" from *Sumac,* reprinted by permission. "The Way It Happens To You," from *Shenandoah* (Summer, 1972), copyright © 1972 by *Shenandoah;* reprinted from *Shenandoah:* The Washington and Lee University Review with permission of the Editor.

VAN K. BROCK. "Lying On A Bridge," from *The Southern Poetry Review* (Spring, Vol. VIII, No. 1.), with permission. "Dead Man Creek" from the *North American Review* (Nov-Dec 1968) copyright © 1968 by the University of Northern Iowa. Reprinted by permission of the author. "The Sea Birds," reprinted by permission; © 1965 by Van K. Brock. Originally in *The New Yorker*. "The Evidence," © 1972 by Van K. Brock, reprinted by permission of the author; originally appeared in the *Georgia Review*.

THOMAS BRUSH. "The Mailman," reprinted by permission of the author. Copyright © 1973 by Thomas Brush. "The Dream of Gerard de Nerval," copyright 1972 by *Shenandoah*, reprinted from *Shenandoah:* The Washington and Lee University Review, with the permission of the Editor. "The Problem With Dreams," from *Poetry Northwest* (Summer, 1971), reprinted by permission of *Poetry Northwest* and the author. "Falling In Love With Tygers," from *Crazy Horse*, reprinted by permission.

RAYMOND CARVER. "Winter Insomnia," "Drinking While Driving," "The Wall," from *Winter Insomnia*. Reprinted by permission of *Kayak*. "Hunter," "Deschutes River," from *Esquire* (November,1971), reprinted by permission of *Esquire* Magazine. Copyright © 1971 by Esquire, Inc.

PETER COOLEY. "The Man Who Closes Himself" from *Trace*, by permission of the Editor of *Trace*. Also appeared in *Poetry Northwest* (Winter, 1970). Reprinted by permission of *Poetry Northwest* and the author. "Ah, Wilderness," copyright 1970 by James Boyerman, originally appeared in *Trace*. "Floating Coathangers," "The White Room," by permission of the author. Copyright © 1973 by Peter Cooley.

SAM CORNISH. "Generations 1," "Frederick Douglass," "Generations 2," "Ray Charles," "Forecast," from *Generations* by Sam Cornish. Copyright © 1968, 1969, 1970, 1971 by Sam Cornish. Reprinted by permission of Beacon Press.

TOM CRAWFORD. "the feeding cycle of the catfish," from *Quarry*. Copyright © 1972 by Quarry and used by permission of the editors. "enormous sleep," from the *North Stone Review*, reprinted by permission. "everything must go," © 1973 by Tom Crawford, reprinted by permission of the author.

PHILIP DACEY. "The Animal's Christmas," from *The New York Times* (12/21/70), copyright © 1970 by The New York Times Company. Reprinted by permission. "The Perfectionist," from the *Westigan Review of Poetry*, reprinted by permission of the *Westigan Review of Poetry*. "Porno Love," reprinted from *The Massachusetts Review*, copyright © 1972 by The Massachusetts Review, Inc. "The Amputee Soldier," first published as "The Wounded Soldier," from the *Westigan Review of Poetry*. Reprinted with permission of the *Westigan Review of Poetry*.

STEPHEN DUNN: "The Loss," from *Poetry Northwest* (Summer, 1971), reprinted by permission of *Poetry Northwest* and the author. "At Every Gas Station There Are Mechanics," reprinted by permission of the author, copyright © 1973 by Stephen Dunn. "Biography In The First Person," from *Poetry Northwest* (Summer, 1971), reprinted by permission of *Poetry Northwest* and the author. "To The Upright," reprinted by permission of *The New Republic*, © 1971, Harrison-Blaine of New Jersey, Inc. "If I Were In Charge of Epiphanies," from *Kayak*, reprinted by permission.

DAVID ALLAN EVANS, "Pole Vaulter," from *Esquire* (November, 1972); reprinted by permission of *Esquire* Magazine, © 1972 by Esquire, Inc. "The Cattle Ghosts," from *Poetry Northwest* (Autumn, 1972), reprinted by permission of *Poetry Northwest* and the author. "Ford Pickup," from *Prairie Schooner* (Winter, 1972-73); copyright © 1973 by The University of Nebraska Press.

"Poem Without A Metaphor," from the *South Dakota Review* (Autumn, 1970), reprinted by permission.

SIV CEDERING FOX. "Hands," from *Crazy Horse*, reprinted by permission. "Ornithology," from the *New York Quarterly*, reprinted by permission. "Poem," from *Dryad*, reprinted by permission.

VIRGINIA GILBERT. "Looking For A Place To Be Comfortable," reprinted by permission of the Back Door Press. "Finding You," from *I Love You All Day/It Is That Simple* by permission of the Abbey Press, St. Meinrad, Indiana. "What Does It Mean, This Harmonica?" reprinted by permission of the author. Copyright © 1973 by Virginia Gilbert.

ROBERT GILLESPIE. "A View Toward Wife Trading," from the *Black Swamp Review*, No. 2, reprinted by permission. "Shawano Lake, Wisconsin," reprinted by permission of the author. Copyright © 1973 by Robert Gillespie. "Snow White," from the *Wisconsin Review* (Vol. 6, No. 2, Spring 1971), reprinted by permission.

ELTON GLASER. "Meal Piece," from *Southern Carolina Literary Scene*, (Vol. 1, No. 3, Feb.-June 1971), reprinted by permission. "The General's Wife," from *Blue Guitar*, reprinted by permission. "Asides and Memoranda," from *Poetry Northwest*, (Summer, 1971), reprinted by permission, of *Poetry Northwest* and the author. "The Sacred Heart of Jesus Bleeds for *You*," from *Crazy Horse*, reprinted by permission.

LOUISE GLÜCK. "The Shad-Blow Tree," "The Fortress," "The Undertaking," from *Poetry* (May, 1971). Copyright © 1971 The Modern Poetry Association. Reprinted by permission of the Editor of *Poetry*. "Gretel in Darkness," from *New American Review*, reprinted by permission.

ALBERT GOLDBARTH. "From The Bridge," reprinted by permission of the author; copyright © 1973 by Albert Goldbarth. "Survival," from *Poetry* (March, 1971). Copyright © 1971 The Modern Poetry Association. Reprinted by permission of the Editor of *Poetry*. "On Sunday, The Beginning of the Week, I Make A Religion," by permission of the *North Stone Review*. "Body Mechanics," from *Skywriting*, vol. 1, no. 1, by permission of the publisher.

MICHAEL S. HARPER. "Breaded Meat, Breaded Hands," from *Field*, reprinted by permission. "Dear John, Dear Coltrane," from the *Carolina Quarterly*, reprinted by permission. "The Black Angel," from *Poetry* (February, 1968), copyright © 1968 by The Modern Poetry Association. Reprinted by permission of the Editor of *Poetry*.

PHILIP HEY. "Epigrams," from *Hearse*, reprinted by permission. "A Thank You Poem For the Andersons," reprinted by permission of the author. Copyright © 1973 by Philip Hey. "Gunfighter," from *Shenandoah* (Summer, 1972); reprinted by permission from *Shenandoah:* The Washington and Lee University Review, with the permission of the Editor.

RON IKAN. "Babylon," "Sidewalk Restoration," "American Saturday Afternoon," reprinted by permission of the author. Copyright © 1973 by Ron Ikan.

ERICA JONG. "The Universal Explicator," from *Poetry* (July,1971), copyright © 1971 The Modern Poetry Association. Reprinted by permission of the Editor of *Poetry*. "The Man Under The Bed," from *Fruits and Vegetables* by Erica Jong. Copyright © 1968, 1970, 1971 by Erica Mann Jong. Reprinted by permission of Holt, Rinehart & Winston, Inc. "Sixteen Warnings In Search Of A Feminist Poem," from *The Nation* (April 5, 1971), with permission of *The Nation*.

R. P. KINGSTON. "He's Known His Lesson For Years," copyright © 1971 by *The Antioch Review,* Inc. First published in *The Antioch Review,* Vol. 31, No. 2, reprinted by permission of the editors. "Mystic Lake," "Between Two Wars," reprinted by permission of the *Kansas Quarterly.* "Stateside," reprinted by permission of the author. Copyright © 1973 by R. P. Kingston.

MAXINE KUMIN. "Morning Swim," copyright © 1962 by Maxine Kumin, "The Pawnbroker," copyright © 1964 by Maxine Kumin, from *The Privilege* by Maxine Kumin. "The Nightmare Factory," from *The Nightmare Factory* by Maxine Kumin, copyright © 1970 by Maxine Kumin. Reprinted by permission of Harper & Row, Publishers, Inc.

GREG KUZMA. "Hose And Iron," from *Poetry* (June, 1970), copyright © 1970 The Modern Poetry Association. Reprinted by permission of the Editor of *Poetry.* "Sleep," "I Visit My Brother," "Ah," copyright © 1970 by *The Antioch Review,* Inc. First published in *The Antioch Review,* Vol. 30, No. 2, reprinted by permission of the editors. "First Camp," from *Field,* reprinted by permission.

LARRY LEVIS. "The Poem You Asked For," "For The Country," "Winter," reprinted from *Wrecking Crew* by Larry Levis by permission of the University of Pittsburgh Press. Copyright © 1971 by the University of Pittsburgh Press.

THOMAS LUX. "If You See This Man," from *Massachusetts Review* (Summer, 1972) reprinted by permission. "Going Home," "Some Oral Stanzas," "Five Men I Know," from *Memory's Handgrenade* by Thomas Lux. Copyright © 1972 by Thomas Lux. Reprinted by permission of the author and Pym-Randall Press. "How To Cure Your Fever," reprinted by permission of the *Emerson Review.*

MORTON MARCUS. "Proverbs," "Family Game," "Hand," from *Origins* by Morton Marcus. Reprinted by permission of *Kayak.* Copyright Morton Marcus. "2 Poems Written On Turning Around Too Quickly While Hiking," from *The Santa Cruz Mountain Poems.* Copyright 1972 by Morton Marcus. Reprinted by permission of Capra Press.

WILLIAM MATTHEWS. "Your Eyes, Your Name," "Praise," from *Sleek For*

The Long Flight by William Matthews. Copyright © 1971, 1972 by William Matthews. Reprinted by permission of Random House, Inc. "Blues For John Coltrane, Dead At 41," Copyright © 1968 by William Matthews. From *Ruining the New Road* by William Matthews. Reprinted by permission of Random House, Inc.

TOM MC KEOWN. "The Buffalo, Our Sacred Beast," from *Drunk All Afternoon,* reprinted by permission of Abraxas Press. "Woman With Finger," from *New Mexico Quarterly* (Winter-Spring, 1969), reprinted by permission. "1937 Ford Convertible," from *Kayak,* reprinted by permission.

WILLIAM PITT ROOT. "The House You Looked For," reprinted by permission of the author. Copyright © 1973 by William Pitt Root. Originally appeared in *Place* magazine. Published 1973 in *Striking the Dark Air for Music* (Atheneum). "Fisherman," "The Jellyfish," from *The Storm and Other Poems* by William Pitt Root. Copyright © 1967, 1968 by William Pitt Root. Reprinted by permission of Atheneum Publishers. "Fisherman" originally appeared in *Hudson Review.* "The Jellyfish," originally appeared in *Massachusetts Review.*

GARY SANGE. "Lighthouse Keeper," reprinted by permission of the author. Copyright © 1973 by Gary Sange. "Truckdriver," "Separation," from *The Quarterly Review of Literature,"* Vol. XVIII, Nos. 1 and 2, reprinted by permission. "Drive In Movie" from *Southern Poetry Review* (Spring, 1966, Vol. VI, No. 2), reprinted by permission.

DENNIS SCHMITZ. "Eclogues," "If I Could Meet God," "The Rabbit Leaves," from *We Weep For Our Strangeness* by Dennis Schmitz. Copyright © 1969 by Dennis Schmitz. Used by permission of Follett Publishing Company, a division of Follett Corporation.

MARY SHUMWAY. "River Road," "Before The Dark Is Down," from *Headlands* by Mary Shumway. Copyright © 1971 by Mary Shumway, reprinted by permission of the author and the Sono Nis Press. "Gooseberry Wine," from *Prairie Schooner* (Fall, 1968). Copyright © 1968 The University of Nebraska Press. "Passage," © 1972 by Mary Shumway; appeared originally in the *Denver Quarterly.* Reprinted by permission.

CHARLES SIMIC. "Butcher Shop," "Poem," "The Wind," "Bones," "Tapestry," "Errata," from *Dismantling the Silence* by Charles Simic; reprinted with the permission of the publisher, George Braziller, Inc. Copyright © 1971 by Charles Simic.

DAVID SMITH. "Mean Rufus Throw-Down," "Dying Off Egg Island Bar," "How One Thing Leads To Another," reprinted with permission from the Basilisk Press.

DAVID STEINGASS. "Midwest U.F.O." "The Seven Year Body Cycle," from *Body Compass* by David Steingass, reprinted by permission of the University of Pittsburgh Press. Copyright © 1969 by the University of Pittsburgh Press.

"Midwest U.F.O." first appeared in the Winter 1968-69 edition of *Poetry Northwest*. "Wisconsin Farm Auction," from *December* (fall issue), reprinted by permission.

LEON STOKESBURY. "To Laura Phelan: 1880-1906," from *The Southern Poetry Review* (Fall, 1971), reprinted by permission. "Summer In Fairbanks," "Back Behind The Eyes," from *Prairie Schooner* (Fall, 1971). Copyright © 1971 by the University of Nebraska Press. "The Graduate Assistant Tells About His Visit," copyright © 1971 by *Shenandoah*, reprinted from *Shenandoah*, The Washington and Lee University Review with permission of the Editor. "Little Keats' Soliloquy," from the *Carolina Quarterly* (Fall, 1969), reprinted by permission.

MARK STRAND. "Elegy For My Father," from *Field* (April, 1972), reprinted by permission. "The Prediction," from *Darker* by Mark Strand. Copyright © 1968, 1970 by Mark Strand. Reprinted by permission of Atheneum Publishers, Inc.

DABNEY STUART. "The Fisherman," "Power Failure," "Hunter, Prey," "His Third Decade," copyright © 1968, 1969 by Dabney Stuart. From *A Particular Place*, by Dabney Stuart. Reprinted by permission of Alfred A. Knopf, Inc.

DENNIS TRUDELL. "39,572," from *Avenues* by Dennis Trudell. Reprinted by permission of Back Cellar Press. Also appeared in *Poetry Northwest* (Spring, 1971). "You Get The Groceries, I'll Guard The Crib," from *Pebble*, copyright © 1970 by Greg Kuzma; reprinted with the permission of *Pebble*. "Epilogue," from *Poetry* (January, 1970), © 1970 by The Modern Poetry Association; reprinted by permission of the Editor of *Poetry*. "I Was Driving . . ." reprinted with permission of *Kumquat*, © The Kumquat Press, 1971.

ALICE WALKER. "Once V," "mornings/ of an impossible love," from *Once*, by Alice Walker, copyright © 1968 by Alice Walker. Reprinted by permission of Harcourt Brace Jovanovich, Inc. "The Old Warrior Terror," from *Revolutionary Petunias* by Alice Walker. Copyright © 1973 by Alice Walker. Reprinted by permission of Harcourt Brace Jovanovich, Inc.

J. D. WHITNEY. "Here," from *sd* by J. D. Whitney, © 1973 by J. D. Whitney, "The Gift," from *The Nabisco Warehouse* by J. D. Whitney, © 1971 by J. D. Whitney. Both poems reprinted by permission of The Elizabeth Press. "Bedtime," from *Crazy Horse*, reprinted by permission.

AL YOUNG. "Squirrels," © 1970 by Al Young, from *Crystalline Flight*, reprinted with permission. "Groupie," © 1971 by Al Young, from *100 Flowers*, reprinted with permission. "Tribute," © 1970 by Al Young, from *Chicago Review*, reprinted with permission. "Loneliness," © 1970 by Al Young, from *Sponge* Magazine, reprinted with permission. These poems appear in a collection entitled *The Song Turning Back On Itself*, published by Holt, Rinehart & Winston in 1971.

James Applewhite

The oldest son of a tobacco farming family, James Applewhite was born in eastern North Carolina in 1935 and holds three degrees from Duke University. After teaching several years at the University of North Carolina at Greensboro, Applewhite now lives in Durham where he teaches at Duke. A winner of the Emily Clark Balch prize, his poems have appeared widely in such publications as: *Shenandoah, New American Review, Poetry, Harper's, The Young American Poets,* and *The American Literary Anthology.* In 1971, with a grant from the North Carolina Council of Arts, he edited a collection of literary writings on the environment called *Voices from Earth.*

MY GRANDFATHER'S FUNERAL

I knew the dignity of the words:
"As for man, his days are as grass,
As a flower of the field so he flourisheth;
For the wind passeth, and he is gone"—
But I was not prepared for the beauty
Of the old people coming from the church,
Nor for the suddenness with which our slow
Procession came again in sight of the awakening
Land, as passing white houses, Negroes
In clothes the colors of the earth they plowed,
We turned, to see bushes and rusting roofs
Flicker past one way, the stretch of fields
Plowed gray or green with rye flow constant
On the other, away to unchanging pines
Hovering over parallel boles like
Dreams of clouds.

                  At the cemetery the people
Surprised me again, walking across
The wave of winter-bleached grass and stones
Toward his grave; grotesques, yet perfect
In their pattern; Wainwright's round head,
His bad shoulder hunched and turning
That hand inward, Luby Paschal's scrubbed
Square face, lips ready to whistle to
A puppy, his wife's delicate ankles
Angling a foot out, Norwood Whitley
Unconsciously rubbing his blue jaw,
Locking his knees as if wearing boots;
The women's dark blue and brocaded black,
Brown stockings on decent legs supporting
Their infirm frames carefully over
The wintry grass that called them down,
Nell Overman moving against the horizon
With round hat and drawn-back shoulders—
Daring to come and show themselves
Above the land, to face the dying
Of William Henry Applewhite,

Whose name was on the central store
He owned no more, who was venerated,
Generous, a tyrant to his family
With his ally, the God of Moses and lightning
(With threat of thunderclouds rising in summer
White and ominous over level fields);
Who kept bright jars of mineral water
On his screened, appled backporch, who prayed
With white hair wispy in the moving air,
Who kept the old way in changing times,
Who killed himself plowing in his garden.
I seemed to see him there, above
The bleached grass in the new spring light,
Bowed to his handplow, bent-kneed, impassive,
Toiling in the sacrament of seasons.

VERSIONS OF SUNLIGHT

I

Driving from Charleston

I ache to touch distance into center of light.
    Herons plane over water, neck-legs longer
  like a kite's staff than wings; crossed sticks in flight,
      that X upon spots they sense, pin bone centers of light.

Stakes of the absolute spectrum seem driven into sawgrass,
    estuarine horizon plated with glitter. Their country
  of whiteness, like ice upon teeth, aches sight. My way
      is the streaming speed makes: asphalt's glints drawing lines,

signposts on pine stands shrinking in the mirror. A man
    cannot enter so wholly in an Other as they live in sunlight.
  I drive with my children and wife. Trips to the beach
      to know sunlight. Once in a motel quick from surf

I stripped off her white wet suit, pushed over upon her white
    backward: desire like the stiffening of a dagger in loins.

Her skin, a few grain-glints of salt, of sand, stung sharp
    in the eye of my skin. That was not this year or last.

Five years, six—have they left me single against distance,
    not even sex for companion? Love moves now on
fields of her body, sees no white sting of sail or wing
    upon distancing water. I dream discoveries on hills I can climb.

II

Reverie on Sunlight

I should walk among second-growth pine, clay heat
    soak of my own sweat for water. I should climb
into the Uwharrie hills   skirt scrub on abandoned farms
    a few oaks standing by chimneys but clouds fast soaking

dreams of the families from crowns' great shadows.
    Washes will follow in flame-wrinkled sand toward
a central heat   I lift to be further alone
    from licks of thundershowers' bolts of water

I will run in a knee high brush   blueberries
    boots sensing snakes' coiled lightning, till the burning
at the bottom of ribs flickers steady to support me
    alone under clouds like an indian   kin

to   children of the rain   and I break vines into the ravine
    where I'm weaker than I think   like a child on lawn
playing swing the statue, as a lip of needles circles me
    yet still when I fall it is face toward the sand

which has funneled around me like mica   perfect
    geometry of glitter   each grain on stem of a splinter
transparent metal   rays from the sun's burst
    molten, and all crumble inward like the hollow

in an hourglass running: to a centering hole   tunnel
    like the burrow of a snake.   This dream I undertake
to attempt   this to accomplish by shifts and dodges
    in bitter-hot fields, inarticulate and real.

In the Uwharrie Hills

I set out in fact. The climb is a tingling
 of blood in arms and legs; I pass cross limbs
left on a stripped pine, like a hawk's perch
 envisioned by a hawk. The log road worn only

by water is rutted too deep for wheels. Pulse knocks
 heady in my ears. I think, watching the Uwharrie hills
from the spine of a basalt rise, old spines in air's smoke:
 this world is charged full of wonders.

An hour ago I broke bushes from the stream's rock
 brink to sun needles funneled around me; fresh from
fearing snakes hidden. Glistening grain by grain
 the golden around me slid from my keeping.

Alive in the middle of act I knew only thirst
 that senses the miracle in a single drink of water,
the dream for a moment idle of sun turned inside its skin
 like a white bird draining to a snake. It nests in the navel of light.

WAR SUMMER

 In our tin-roofed house in the big war's summer,
 In a somnolent town in sunlight's dominion,
 I read of the Shalotte of Lord Tennyson,
 Dreaming beyond guardrooms of a distant thunder
 To a city in that sun's blind center.

 How odd in my upstairs room, awake
 In attic air, in wrath of the sun,
 Except for my balsa Spitfire, alone,
 Unable to descend, where my father'd mistake
 My desire as he massed his jaws at steak.

 Would ardor of sunflame never relent?
 My thoughts were a web as in the Lady's tower.

Tinkering tissue and sticks toward the power
Of flight, I dreamed all communion as ascent.
Our rapport in combat came only at twilight.

Through rumble of distant thunder, far
Flash of the six o'clock news. Under each
Portentous cloud, we turned from our workbench
Stunned. Radio's tone warned static; came roar
Above houses, artillery of a wide atmosphere.

DREAM OF ASCENT

Through a blue-buoyant lake of air wavers
The wrinkled vastness of the mountain valley.
Filaments radiate from our fingertips, web us
To the sun's magnetic beams. My son
Is behind me, the arrow of his breastbone
Is aimed with mine. We have passed over
The cities of men, I know soon the dream will change,
But now for a moment we soar, tasting
With our breasts and our limbs
The billows of ascent.

Wires crisscross the skyline and flight
Is the motion of a car. We slide along streets of a city
We've lived in before, where the whiteness of houses seems sight.
We are known and awaited; it only remains
For me to recognize from the incredibly
Quick blur of scenes from my past which rush by
Unseen by the others, like a secret locomotive
Rushing inside façades of the roadside,
The look which will signal our turning.

Then the one face has flashed and I turn, follow
A narrow alley until the car is motionless
On a sloped earth yard where the fall leaves blow
And are heaped against fenders. I can see
From inside myself the rooms which are contained
In the house beside us. White and old.

Grooved boards. The stairway rises, the worn carpet
Has in its pattern skeined smoke,
Birds of paradise quick within vines.

The door opens into a room
With made bed smooth as the snow over hummocks.
The walls are blue, phase into the dimension
That deep sky shows through its individual
Squares of glass. Over the bed hangs
A portrait smoked by time.
I turn to catch my son;
His arms are about my waist.
I don't wish him to see it yet
I am not ready (unworthy and afraid) to be for him
That countenance deep as space between boles of a winter
Forest in its gilt frame, through the darkened glass.

ON "VERSIONS OF SUNLIGHT"

The poem began, I believe, as I walked along the battery at Charleston.
A gull flashed into water far across the river, or perhaps it was a sudden
whitecap broken by that exhilarating wind. I felt over again, for the
hundredth or thousandth time an old sensation of desire; there, the
wind hollowing my body, I ached with the pang of that gull or white
wave, nostalgic for the infinite.

But the poem was not to be one of limitless, therefore ineffectual,
seeking. It was to be one of the emotions and imagination instructed by
events and limits. Half in my mind as I walked was the memory of a
former trip when my wife and I had stopped at that same white Hotel
Fort Sumpter on the point of the battery. It had been enough years ago
that sex had seemed then as aching and breathless a distance of desire as
that gull across the river. Then we had traveled alone. But next day as we
drove along the coast homeward through an incredible intensity of sun-
light, we had about us our three children, fruits of the years between the
first trip and this. The gull and its longing was regenerated for me in
herons which flew over and waded the glittering reaches of estuary and
marsh. I meditated on this seeking they triggered, which was like our
rushing toward a horizon that receded, like my former desire, which I
realized had changed. Time had changed that. Now I loved my wife
only, not some horizon image of brightness I sensed through her body.

So there arose in imagination a version of a trip toward the white
secret which should suit my present life. I saw it was to be a trip on foot,

not sailing across water and yearning toward flight, but climbing upon hills my own legs could master. I climbed in imagination over the scrub-pine Uwharrie range, geologically one of the oldest in America, but worn now to hills of no spectacular dimension. Still the excitement of pushing toward a final destination took hold of me and I imagined myself running in a sunlight as blistering as what fell about us as we drove. I saw that my destination would be a clearing in pines, white sand funneled in the center, sand as if connected each grain by each to a million indivisible needles of sunlight. I saw that this crystallization of white out of the spectrum crumbled inward like sand in an hourglass draining, that it funneled toward a hole. That would be the navel, door into the center of sunlight. It looked curiously like the burrow of a snake. We had seen in a museum in Charleston an exhibit, with paintings and stuffed birds, on the evolution of reptiles into flight. But a snake is in imagination a dweller in darkness, and I had been called to this search by the brilliance of plumage in sunlight. Did my reverie say that a trip to the center of light must pass into darkness? I resolved, upon arriving home, to go to the Uwharrie hills and try my dream against the fact.

In a couple of days I drove the fifty or so miles southward to the Uwharrie hills. It was in a sense a dangerous experiment. What one of us has not feared that the fact must always pale beside the dream, that experience cannot live up to imagination?

I couldn't find a landscape quite as I had imagined it. In desperation I stopped my car beside a stream, crossed it, and plunged into the tangled brush. The heat was entirely satisfactory. I thrashed about for an hour or more, crossing the stream several times on its rocks, but chiefly held from free movement by the tangle of vegetation along its banks. Finally I pushed by main force through a wall of branches, my ankles feeling endangered by snakes, into an abandoned logging trail. As I drank from the canteen, water to my thirst and sun upon the sweat of face seemed all that I could want.

The trail led back to the paved road. No cars came along it, only the clouds rubbing closely over trees. I decided to run along the road. I'd run as far as I was able in the heat, then see what.

When breathing was licking about the bottom of my ribs like a fire the road dipped through a valley, I crossed a bridge, felt the sweetness of a very small meadow, then saw a rutted clay trail starting to my right up a rise. I took it. The incline stopped my lope immediately. I climbed, keeping to a pace that suspended me just this side of exhaustion. I heard the blood thumping in my ears.

The "hawk's perch" was actual. It was in a clearing where lumbering had taken place several years ago, and the peeled sapling, still rooted, ended in a perfect small cross. I don't know how it could have been peeled and left upright.

Water from thundershowers must have ripped down the road's slope like lightning. Washes were gouged steeply into a clay red as flames. Finally near the crest of what had proved a small mountain I came upon a view where all of the Uwharrie hills heaved their leaf-glittering backs into view through a smoke of clear air like folds of some primordial snake emerging from the water. I was satisfied.

I meditated and wrote the poem's first draft over the next several days. The last version of the experience came to me in writing, or, rather, while walking outside under moving cloud shadows, thinking about the writing. I had been to a final point, as far as I was able to travel given the terrain and heat. On the mountain, or earlier, by the stream, drinking from my canteen, were moments gone deeply into memory, but yet not permanent centers. They were circles, moments close enough to the navel of sunlight that in their stillness I could sense its motion. Was the miracle of any sight or sensation indissoluble from the slipping of its needles?

Snakes regenerate, slip out of their skins in darkness and come again. If the call of the white bird was to a destination I should reach only at the end of living, I was no longer in a hurry. I should like to enjoy the outward flanks and fur-sheen of sun for quite a time longer. Weigh its grains in my palm, golden because slipping through my fingers.

Coleman Barks

Coleman Barks was born in 1937 in Chattanooga, Tennessee. He has B.A. and Ph.D. degrees from the University of North Carolina, and an M.A. from the University of California at Berkeley. After having taught at the universities of North Carolina and Southern California, Barks presently teaches in the English Department of the University of Georgia in Athens. A widely published writer, his poems have appeared in publications such as: *Chelsea, Red Clay Reader, Tennessee Poetry Journal, Carolina Quarterly*, and *Fiddlehead*, and in anthologies such as: *Quickly Aging Here: Some Poets of the 1970's, Pith and Vinegar*, and *New Generation: Poetry*. His first collection of poems, *The Juice*, was published in 1972 by Harper & Row.

FROM *BODY POEMS*

Downy Hair in the Shape of a Flame
Moving up the Stomach and End-
ing at the Solar Plexus

anything this
recognizable

should have
a name:

*   *   *

White Crescents at the Bottoms
of Fingernails and
Toenails

the edge of
a coat-of-arms:

who do you think you are

*   *   *

Adam's Apple

never said
a word:

he just nodded

*   *   *

Achilles Tendon

walk on your heels
across a puddle:

you mythological
beast

* * *

Tic

talk to me
talk to me

* * *

Genitals

the loaded question

the slick answer

* * *

Semen

thousands
of weird little figurines
carved out of soap

suddenly come alive
and jabber like
foreigners

* * *

Cheek

somebody's hiding
in the drapes
I bet I know who:

No   it's just his shoes

* * *

Brain

a flashlight
looking through the empty
limbs

* * *

Skull

a folk remedy
for the lovesick:

share a meal
of turtle meat

then tack the shell up
for a birdhouse

* * *

Scar

the one chance
I will ever have
to go to Finland

is a long lake
frozen to my leg

* * *

Back Just Below the Shoulder Blades

the most kissed
stone tablet
at a sacred grotto:

the one nearest
where it happened

* * *

Dimple

a saltlick
for deer

From *Body Poems* 13

* * *

Skeleton

on this jungle gym

* * *

Liver

a dripping locker room
full of older men

* * *

Bruises

paint samples

* * *

Hair on the Chest

cash on the barrelhead
(who'll cover my bet)

* * *

ON "BODY POEMS"

I have always liked the way some poems travel through the body and
seem to require a physical response. Keats rising up from his chair,
hunching his shoulders when he reads Spenser's phrase, *the sea-shoul-
dering whales.* Such kinesthetic energy is essential to poetry, I think, and
the image most often serves as the conductor for this energy. Bodily re-
sponse to images is what I'm after in these short poems. The minnow
inside the wrist, the dice in the ankles, the limbs in the limbs. In fact,
this sequence began almost as calisthenics, as an exercise, a meditation
on the parts of the body and the way they contain bits of landscape,
animals, memories, losses, jokes, the seeds of our death, and someone

else's birth. But mainly at first trying to practice a quick, immediate touch between words and reader. Now, though, the poems seem to be moving toward more inclusive sensations, like the sense of the body's symmetry, its hollowness and resonance, and the feel of the whole figure moving. The sequence itself, up to over a hundred poems now, is not concerned with making a statement, or with being complete, or completed. Though it is concerned with going somewhere, as my sense of my own body moves and tries to understand.

Some comment on individual sections. *Skull*—Turtles are sacred animals for me, like spirits from the lake I grew up close to. I've never made a birdhouse from a turtleshell, but I like the idea, the way the elements of air and water are balanced in the image. Sailors believe that turtle-meat is an aphrodisiac. It's not, but they believe it. *Liver*—A reminder of my father's sitting there in the locker room, that I carry around with me. *Tic*—An eye's morse code. *Adam's Apple*—Consent, with a voicebox stuck in the craw. *Achilles Tendon*—Her hold, the water's hold, upon the body. *Shadow*—Another one of her shapes. *Downy Hair.* etc.—Whoever put names on the body has done a beautiful job so far. Think of *shoulder blades*, or *cowlick*. Why not name the rest?

Marvin Bell

Marvin Bell was born in 1937 in New York City and grew up in Center Moriches—half-way out on the south shore of Long Island. He attended Alfred University, Syracuse, the University of Chicago, and the University of Iowa, where he is currently an Associate Professor and a member of the Writers' Workshop staff. His poems have appeared widely in magazines and anthologies. A winner of the Emily Clark Balch Prize in 1970 as well as the Lamont Poetry Award for 1969 for his book, *A Probable Volume of Dreams* (1969), he is also the author of *Things We Dreamt We Died For* (1966), Poems for Nathan and Saul (1966), *Woo Havoc* (1971), and *The Escape Into You* (1971).

IN THE HOME

Nothing in thick clothes is
happening, no grounds for divorce
this time, no one breaking down the
last rung in the ladder of lusts
propped against the house of bonafide fidelity
no one can enter but must prove residence.

If a step on the stair
is a fist in the heart,
if one treads carefully
on the ego and the heart in the hand,
if the song in your heart is my heart
in your mouth—why, that's bloody possible.

What's a metaphor but a mask,
a conceit but a god-awful bore?
Either/or: there's more to be said for slumber
after a good screw: turning in for the night:
with more than a handful of pleasure,
with more than oneself to come to.

AMERICAN POETS

Vision doesn't mean anything real
for most of them. They dance
beautifully way out on the thin limbs
at the top of the family tree,
which we have admired for
its solid trunk and unseen roots

we know go back to other countries
where "God help us" was a prayer
one planted like a seed, staking everything
on labor, luck and no concessions.
All of us remember the rains that year
which exhausted the Czar and the Bolsheviks.

Hungry, wet, not yet sick of ourselves,
we escaped by parting the waters;
we brought this black bread to live on,
and extra enough for a child.
That bread didn't grow on trees.
We multiplied, but we didn't reproduce.

SONG: THE ORGANIC YEARS

Love, if nothing solid rises like wood
above this scratching, this waxen cane
of a tree, if nothing from this trunk
unflowers after long reaching, if finally
the leaf relaxes its bodily processes,
at least we had a hand out to help it.

Also, you have carried me far on your
way into the earth, in the prophetic
imagery of your tunnels I was satisfied,
and in your lovely arms I lay weeping
the truth. If belief doesn't make up
for the long argument of life, still

we made up with what was natural. Now,
from the long, blind alleys of learning,
and in the winter of metaphor, our arms
reach like branches toward the light, our
roots go down to clear water, our fingers,
so long counted on, are not dry yet.

HER DREAM HOUSE

Birds cannot fly over it.
It is only as tall as I dictate.
One word from me, and the windows
open good-naturedly, doors close

off the unused rooms, or perhaps
the cellar loses its water.
I should imagine it would do
what imitations I tell it to;
I shall possess it.
And in it we will tend to
the doing of the days
with a new sense of righteousness.
O all the order by accident—
the coverings and the pretty pictures,
the authenticity of the materials!
And O the penny-color pronouncements!
I shall work its makers hard
to create an approving environment
for whatsoever I may choose
or henceforth be seized by.
Hereafter, let fantasy be exposed
for a common denominator.
For I shall live in this house
as the actress of my dreams,
in a house that invites my playing.
And I shall be the first instance
of health, gathering my split dreams
under the flag of abandonment.
In a house which loves you,
all things are possible.

THE DELICATE BIRD WHO IS FLYING
UP OUR ASSES

The delicate bird who flies up your asses
is flying up mine
also, with no express invitation.
The bird who likes the lean and hungry
is making me sweat.
I have delusions that I need a job,
that I will waste away
unless I eat the bird,

and that my family will remember me
only as a poor provider.
That bird means to straighten me out.
The bird in favor of fathers and sons
is cropping up insidiously.
Once I could be lazy;
now he turns up everywhere I sit.
Each day I have a feeling of the bird
higher within me.
Once I declined burdens;
now I jump to be responsible
for ones I haven't yet.
I can tell that bird
means to stay with me forever.
Hire me. I have another mouth to feed.

ON "IN THE HOME," "AMERICAN POETS," "SONG: THE ORGANIC YEARS"

["In the Home," "American Poets," and "Song: The Organic Years" are three in a fifty-four poem sequence, *The Escape Into You*, which I believe is my best, as well as most urgent, work published to date. The history of it which I offer here is honest but incomplete. Poet or poem? Life or art?]

Looking through worksheets in May of 1968, I became interested once more in poems titled "I Adore You" (1960) and "The Ring"—both written four months earlier. They held a fatal attraction for me—partly "formal," partly emotional. They seemed a possible form for discovery, a way to something one couldn't see. Moreover, slowly I became aware that I had not previously considered the poems "finished" only because they had seemed both complete and incomplete.

At first, I set out to do more in the form—concentrating, for the moment, only on the intensity and intimacy I had seen in the first two. (Later, I would realize that I had been writing out of panic.) I completed two more.

Next, I tried consciously to extend the content of the first four. But these several additional poems turned out badly. Thus corrected, I went back to trusting my materials to lead me to "meaning," hoping to recognize it when it revealed itself. Gradually, it became clear to me that I was writing a "love sequence"; later, I realized it would become a book. (I should add that I was fairly determined not to encourage it, if at all possible, to become more than a book, since I felt that both the aesthetic and content could be worked through and discovered, respectively, within one volume—of perhaps sixty poems.)

The sequence was, in large measure, sexual—naturally. It was domestic and anti-domestic—also naturally. "Love," for this book, included love, hate, sex, marriage and divorce, and more. I found, also, that I was writing political poems—i.e., poems of what used to be called "social concern"—and *that s*eemed natural too, if the community is an extension of the family, and the family an extension of any one-to-one relationship.

I continued writing these short poems until I felt I had exhausted the form for the time being and had discovered three "aspects" of the subject matter: narrative, emblematic, and argumentative. I had completed at least twice as many of these poems as would eventually go into the book. As it happened, I had written perhaps forty-four of those I would save during the first two years, 1968 and 1969. Throughout 1970, I had written poems almost exclusively for the final section of the book—the poems in which I sensed that what had gone before would now permit new combinations of truth and affirmation. I found that, for the most part, ordering followed chronology. Poems written about the same time tended to sound more similar to one another than to others, and properly went together for the sake of narrative and argument.

The poems in this sequence proved emotionally expensive. My tendency was to want to pay the cost all at once. But I could not. Instead, I held onto the manuscript, long after I probably could have shaped it into a book. I think I wanted to be sure the book was done. Eventually, I realized that the distance between this particular set of poems and my life at the time was not very great, and that, since the life was not over (nor even the preoccupations of the time), the book would have to be shaped accordingly. Thus, I ended the book, not with a poem, but with a statement from *The Talmud*, from the Sayings of the Fathers: "It is not incumbent upon you to complete this task;/ neither are you free to desist from it." That seemed to me true. Yet the truth in it neither precluded me from publishing this book, nor from moving to the next thing. The book appeared in August, 1971.

"In the Home" is about making, and missing, love; "American Poets" is about making, and missing, poems that matter; and "Song: The Organic Years" is about making peace with death. They share defiance. Like most of the poems in the sequence, they put portions of one's life under intense pressure, as if the skull might be a vise, then screw the threads tighter.

A woman in San Francisco, having just heard some of the early poems in the sequence, told me, "These poems are like an eye—evading, evading. There is something it doesn't want to see. And then there is a moment in each poem in which the eye looks and sees and the poem bursts through to its real subject." That seemed to me a fair description then of my tendency to abandon myself to the materials, *up to a point*. And it still does.

As to the individual poems, I wanted each to be both surprising and inevitable at every turn. Why not? It seemed to me the fundamental demand, perhaps never to be wholly satisfied, which we have placed both on art and life.

One more remark. I had reasons, not plans.

Harold Bond

Born in 1939 in Boston, Mass. Harold Bond has degrees from North-
eastern University, Boston and the University of Iowa. He has held
various editorial positions in magazine, newspaper, and book publishing,
and at present is director of the poetry workshop at the Cambridge
Center for Adult Education. A winner of several literary awards, his
poems have appeared in *The New Yorker, Saturday Review, Harper's,*
and *The New Republic,* and in many anthologies of contemporary Amer-
ican poetry. His books are *The Northern Wall* (1969), *Dancing on Water*
(1970), and *Fragments of an Earlier Life* (1973).

IT IS OREGON, THE HIGHWAY LOOMS

It is Oregon, the highway looms
ahead of me like a phantom telescope.
The ocean is shimmering,

the ocean is a picture postcard
shimmering in expectation of my arrival.
I have removed my clothing,

I am sunbathing under a seacliff.
A fiddler crab sashays over the sand dunes.
It is parked on my belly,

it is being cooked by the hot sun
on my belly. Seagulls are watching me
devour the crustacean,

the crustacean is so huge I will use
its shell for the missing hubcap on my car.
The seagulls have flown away,

the seagulls were nauseated, they were
my only friends. Balboa, riderless surfboards
are coming in on the tide.

Behind me the slim, weekend voyeurs
are beside themselves. My suitcase is bulging
with daisies. I will drive on

to San Francisco. Words are flammable,
juices flow. Crossing bridges, I will revere
silence as my only plan.

GIRLS WHO WAVE AT CARS FROM BRIDGES

You have seen them. Above the freeways
they hang from bridges, their velvet eyes

yielding secrets which you cannot know.
They wave to you hello and goodbye.

They wave this one time and forever.
They wave at old men who no longer

believe girls wave at them from bridges.
Sleek-finned convertibles drag and cruise

and bargain for a spot below them.
You look up, and you can see through them.

Their faces are creampuffs; their skirts are
so high their billowing hair appears

as streamers on a skyful of kites.
Were you to reach up and seize their white

ankles, their lithe, exquisite ankles,
you could spin them on the antenna

of your car. And were they to reach down
and cup their hands lightly on your chin,

they would fly off with you. Together
you would be a solid bet, a sure

pie in the sky. You would touch their noses,
and they would whisper to you what they know.

THE WAY IT HAPPENS TO YOU

Leaving, to where it was that
I was going, I cocked my tongue deep
inside my cheek. Arleta, California
was swirling around me
like an ocean. My rear-view mirror
grew amniotic, my shirt sleeve
became a pearl, brilliant and probable.

Leaving, I left only to return.
The myriad little second
cousins washed back into view,
a seascape of ragdolls fluttering above
the waves. For half the day
I had driven the maximum distance,
returning, at night, to Arleta, California.

So it was I spent as much
time leaving as returning, each day,
each morning, by dint of leaving sooner
instead of later, arriving closer
to where it was that I was going,
before returning, by nightfall,
to Arleta, California.

So it was until I left so early
I saw myself returning
from the night before. This was the day
that I would be arriving
beyond the maximum possible distance.
The myriad little second cousins
would flutter below the browbeating waves;

and turning over in her bed of water,
her tongue uncocked, across America
the woman, awakening only
to mark the time on a calendar
so beautiful she will keep it forever,
would hear my footsteps, and hear
the brilliant pearl dropping outside her door.

ON "IT IS OREGON, THE HIGHWAY LOOMS"

This poem attempts to externalize one experience of aloneness in relation to the factors manipulating that experience. Structurally, the poem is developed along conventional lines with a beginning (the arrival, in travel, along the ocean), a middle (the happenings under the seacliff), and an ending (the anticipated departure, which anticipates, again, another arrival). Thematically, the intent also is not unconventional. All that individualizes the experience of aloneness, or alienation, is the identity of the images developed through the poem. Although it easily could be only another twentieth-century complaint, the poem is heightened, hopefully, by the particularizing of images in counterpoint with the speaker.

The images are twofold, and just as they play off against the speaker, they also play off against one another. There are, first, the reluctant artifacts: automobile trappings (the highway, the hubcap image), surfboards (which, though riderless, continue to come in on the tide), and the suitcase (which is packed with calculated goodwill). Secondly, there are the prospective violators of the speaker's aloneness: the fiddler crab, which is promptly eaten, and the seagulls, which are driven away by the sight below them. In addition to these, the one image of man, aside from the speaker, is that of the "weekend voyeurs"—the nonparticipants, or the observers, as in the seagull image. Through both aspects of the latter images—man and nonman—the intent is to suggest that the speaker's aloneness is at least partly self-wrought and partly not.

The poem begins to shift in the second to last stanza with the statement "My suitcase is bulging with daisies." In the last stanza the poem, for the first time, departs from the heavy image orientation of the rest of the poem. Whatever strength the two closing declarative sentences have is achieved through the context of what preceded them, and whatever reckoning may have occurred in the poem is suggested here—perhaps that, as words fail, daisies may do.

Van K. Brock

Van K. Brock has M.A., M.F.A., and Ph.D. degrees from the University of Iowa, and since 1970 has taught at The Florida State University in Tallahassee. His poems have appeared in *Yale Review, North American Review, Prairie Schooner*, and *Shenandoah,* as well as in anthologies such as the Borestone Mountain Poetry Award's *Best Poems of 1965* and *Best Poems of 1971, Southern Writing of the Sixties: Poetry,* and *The New Yorker Book of Poetry.* A collection of his poems, *Final Belief,* was published by the Back Door Press in 1972.

LYING ON A BRIDGE

We saw anchored worlds in a shallow stream.
The current tugged at clouds, the sun, our faces.
And while we stared, as though into a dream,
The stream moved on; the anchors kept their places.
Even the white rose thorned into your hair
Stayed there, though its refracted, scattered aura
Circled your abstract face, like snow in air;
Then the rose fell onto that gentle water,
Shattering our faces with their mirror. But sun
And clouds, and all their height and depth of light,
Could not feel so involved, nor watch when one
Bloom touched that current and waltzed it out of sight.
Though rising, we saw how all things float in space:
The stars and clouds, ourselves, each other's face.

DEAD MAN CREEK

The water was usually clean
where the river backed upstream
to receive Dead Man Creek,
but we swam out and dived
from anchored inner tubes
for tires, luggage and books.
Skins sealed with semen
floated. Gar, cottonmouth
and gators were sighted. Once
we netted a bloated human
fetus out fingers dissolved
at touch. But I still have
John Brown's Body, The Aeneid
(in stilted English), and one
work in the original Greek.

We hung a tire from a limb
over the cove, dried
the books in a driftboard

treehouse, and swung above
the water. We fished with hooks
and nets (gloved hands for cats),
then afterward washed in the stream
beneath the waterfall
and ate our kill and catch,
telling dirty jokes,
talking of cock like virgins.
By a sinking sun we dredged
enormities from each other
with stories: I remember the panthers
crouching in dark shadows
(half-cat, half-human; no way
to tell the real), swaying
with limbs and sounding like beautiful
women distressed. Waiting.
Wanting to bring you to them.
We believed it all. Each
heard the sound in himself.
So real was Albert's scream
that a startled mockingbird picked up
the cry from the telling to make
a song of our terror, repeating
it purely, repeatedly. Those nights
we headed home, sure
that we would not get there,
weighing the penalties.

THE SEA BIRDS

No light except the stars, but from the cliff
I saw in motion, out on the rolling waves,
The white sea birds that swim beyond the surf.

Their movements made a pattern on the mauve,
Contorted stretch of cold, corrosive water,
Where even the images of stars dissolve.

When I had thought the birds were fixed in order,
I saw the swimming rim of their starlit ring
Minutely swerve and spiral toward the center:

The birds that had been swimming in between
Were shuttled outward on a wheel of light,
Reflecting, like the sea, the star's design.

I paused, and looked, and saw a star burn out
And sink back into space as through a fissure.
It was an ancient word without a thought.

Perhaps birds move in pattern for the measure
It imposes on the ruptured waves at night;
Perhaps they spiral purely for their pleasure.

While I was trying to untie this knot,
A motion in the motion of the weather
Turned, and the birds turned too and tore the net

I knitted for them (a star had torn another
I had knitted for stars). I saw them climb the gale
That drove small arrows in through every feather—

One by one they spread their flapping sails.
I think the stars are moving in a school
With restless birds above a freezing pool,
And no one shall put salt on their bright tails.

THE EVIDENCE

My son kept wanting a snake.
That day our walk went
to a wooded hill
near the school,
where we found on a winding path,
suddenly widening,

the burned and shrivelled
plastic flesh
of toy men among
thirty or forty long
wooden match stems,
red-and-white heads charred
though few burnt after
the first spurt of fire
startled nervous hands.
The evidence lay there,
almost looking unstruck,
surrounding
soldiers dressed for a battle
more real than themselves,
several fused in a mass.
Here and there, others,
apart, were
equally deformed.
Among them, unharmed,
was a lone survivor
and, beside him, one match
unstruck. I let my son
bring the survivor home
and kept the match.
We found no snake,
But a symbol as innocent in itself
And as dreadful in his delight.
Now it is late,
the neighborhood is still,
I sit in the living room,
run my thumbnail
through the match's head
and watch it spurt
white, blue, red
and go out.
It doesn't help.
As light after light goes out
in the thousand houses around me
a child is striking
matches in his sleep.

ON "DEAD MAN CREEK"

Few successful poems are made by a prior formula. Any account of a poem's origin must indulge in what Kenneth Burke calls "prophesying after the fact." It is difficult to separate what one has previously *intended* from what one afterwards seems to have done, for the real *intention* of the poem is what the poet discovers in the process of composition, if he is a competent reader of his own work and can accurately judge his own motives. "Dead Man Creek" reached far back into my experience, in part to early childhood, for its emotion, and it had gestated in the limbo of my intentions for several years before I tried to evoke that half-magical, mythic consciousness of childhood where the animal and human and the natural and supernatural interpenetrate. The poem is concerned with that landscape which more or less culminates with puberty and its rituals. The title is complex, suggesting things unrevealed while referring to both the clean stream of youth, irretrievably lost, and the polluted river which absorbs it.

Talking with Guy Owen [poet, novelist, teacher at North Carolina State University, Raleigh] one night in 1967 about folklore, I told him the story of the panthers and mentioned planning to use it in a poem. His challenge got me started. The swimming hole, as a central pastoral image of boyhood, provides a convenient focus for the concentration of childhood experience which is both purged and more fearfully confronted in the story of the panther. Since adults embody the reality principle, children enter their own world of fantasy most eerily alone with each other (which is to say, in the wild). In the backwash of this river the freshness of nature meets the pollution of civilization in concrete ways. The child is likely to have such encounters there. I remember one adult in our community whose primary interest in swimming was the opportunity it afforded him to tease boys about their sexual organs. There are a number of such nexuses in the poem. The children are approaching the age of independence and decision. They have acquired and recreated the rudiments of society. They both fear and strain toward independence from home and the frightening choices children must sometimes make alone. The swimming hole impinges on the river somewhat as the private unconscious impinges on the archetypal. That the child encounters various perversions of adult society and its symbols here means there is no place where he will not. Finally, he is equally afraid of going home and getting lost—the penalties are ultimately the same. He must risk the world and, at least in some way, accept it.

The story of the panthers was current in rural South Georgia and North Florida when I was a child (and is still found there) though the pumas that had once inhabited that area, and which were called panthers, had long since been pushed westward or southward. I doubt that even the older people could remember a panther in that area. They never told of having seen one. The panther in the poem is a phantom objectification of the boy's fears. The boy knows there are no panthers in the woods, which makes them more frightening since he can never encounter them or dispel his fear of their being there. He can only encounter his fear and dispel it in his stories, in the sublimation and catharsis of art. And this is what he tries to do. But in objectifying it in art, it becomes a real part of nature, as Albert's scream becomes part of the song of the mockingbird. These repetitions are endless, like the movement toward civilization through the catharsis and sublimation of experience. Albert is probably an adult friend of mine, a philosopher living in N.Y.C., who is inside himself a fusion of Huck Finn and Holden Caulfield.

At some point in the early stages of working out this poem, I made a conscious decision to use accentual trimeter, a metrical form which commits the poet to three accents in every line with a varying number of overall syllables per line. Because I decided not to use regular end-rhyme, I tried to achieve a greater density of phonetic repetition within lines, using alliteration, consonance, assonance, internal rhyme and occasional end-rhyme. Diametrically counter to regular stanzaic division, I made the lines run-on in a continuous progression. Altogether these chosen formal stances should seem straightforward, casual, and unposed and contribute probability to the sort of authentic talking voice I felt important for the poem. Twelve-year-olds, after all, are tough realists to deal with and must be evoked on their own terms. And it's not a matter of which form to use but how. The old form-freedom issue is largely simplistic anyway, for while it is adherence to the forms and cadences of language (as recorded in the experience of the ear) that makes a poem viable metrically, form can be as substance to the sensitivity of the poet. But the free play *within* the accentual trimeter form can remind us, if it succeeds, that art proceeds from a calculated risk taken with formlessness.

Thomas Brush

Thomas Brush was born in Yakima, Washington in 1941 and received a B.A. in English and a B.A. in Education from Central Washington State College. He received his M.A. in Creative Writing from the University of Washington where he studied under the writers Tony Connor, David Wagoner, and Jack Cady. Presently he is teaching at Kent-Meridian High School in Kent, Washington.

THE MAILMAN

He has been walking toward me for a thousand miles, on the edge
Of dark streets, across lawns where sprinklers melt in the grass,
Through Saturday nights sprawled in the gardens and cloudy
Sunday mornings, around the howling dogs that leap for him. And I
Have fallen in love with him, with his great leather pouch, slung
On his shoulder like a bride, his shoes that squeak for blocks,
The uniform stained with sweat, from what he carries to bring me
Life, with his eyes shining like candles in the dark, lighting
His face, the cheekbones glowing like polished stone, the hollow
Where his mouth should be, with his silence. And after years of rain
On advertisements, Acapulco in the snow, the sun on the Alps, and
Certificates of my birth, a wedding announcement so I would know
Her name, he brings my death, and one goodbye.

GERARD de NERVAL

". . . and when, one day, he was found in Palais-Royal, leading a lobster at the
end of a ribbon (because, he said, it does not bark, and knows the secrets of the
sea), the visionary had simply lost control of his visions, and had to be sent to
Dr. Blanche's asylum at Montmartre."

—Arthur Symons

It is always morning. The fields of Europe begin to dissolve. Everywhere
Paris is dark and wet. The cafes are closed against the rain, and the heavy
Wooden shutters begin to break open. Late March began in the sea, and I
Must find what it was. In the bright caves on the ocean floor, with ribbons
Shining like water, pouring from my hands. There are so many things to
    know.

There are strange cities, falling all around me. The bars are filling
With Arabs and English. Old women sell fruit and cigars in the streets.
I keep looking for the girl I love. But no one knows who I am. A man
Who says I must come with him, leads me away. All afternoon

Roaches grow from the thick, gray walls, and from the barred windows
    I look
At the sea, at the people of Normandie, who carry silk handkerchiefs,
And walk, whole crowds of them, into this cell, to drown.

THE PROBLEM WITH DREAMS

The problem is to leave the dreams
Behind, to let sleep like rain
Pour from your head, leave the pillows
Yawning where the blankets have been,
Get up on two feet nodding your way
From morning through a hazy afternoon,
Keep your eyes open with the sun rising
On the edge of your face.

Step down out of your wishes
And prepare for a trip, with hats
To keep the shadows inside, a heavy
Coat to keep the cold in, boots to your knees
Will let you know where you're going, wear dark
Glasses and stay away from mirrors.

Let hope, like leaves, slip from your mind,
Avoid novels without endings, stay away from late shows,
Run through your lectures with snow on your feet,
Have drifts in your pockets, with luck
You'll never have to use them.

But keep a wish
Deep in your mind as in a suitcase.
You never know when you'll run out
Of reality.

FALLING IN LOVE WITH TYGERS

They are coming through the bright fields,
Walking on the soft edge of the moon,
With their heads down, quietly through the melting light,
With their eyes closed, dreaming of what went before, the moving
Trees and the gray birds floating just above the ground, with water
Flowing out of the softening grass, and you will
Not believe it, until you lie with them, removing
What's in the way, the face you've made.

Gerard de Nerval 37

And if you do that, you will forever approach barns carefully,
Walk quietly toward sheds, be alert in open pastures, beware
The dogs before the flying hearth lest they come too close,
With eyes burning and tongues dripping, kneeling beside you, telling
You their dreams, what happened, what is possible.
They will fold the darkness behind you.

ON "GERARD DE NERVAL"

This poem came out of two separate experiences. The second was, of course, the Symons chapter on Gerard de Nerval, in *The Symbolist Movement in Literature,* and the first, about which I have written a number of poems and which has yet to leave me alone, concerns a man I know very well, who is I think, much like Gerard. He has now gone mad, and is in a hospital for the insane. He lived on "skid row" (the city is unimportant) for the past few years and like Gerard would frequently lapse into fantasy. I must continue to write about him, his friends and his haunts, and the Symons article set up, what was for me, a corresponding figure. Like Gerard he had moments of brilliance and, while not a poet, would often speak of visions, mixing them with history and philosophy both real and imagined, and with the failures and successes of those he met and knew in the taverns, bars and flop houses where he lived. And near the end, when he lived in alleys, smoked cigarets rolled in newspaper, and ate popcorn to swell his stomach against hunger, he told me he would soon leave for the coast and sunshine. The last time I saw him, he was in the institution and would remain there, or so the doctor told me. And it seems to me that his imaginary journey to the sea and his vision of his life, past and present, could be much like Gerard's search for his unattainable love and life. What, I suppose, this adds up to is an attempt, through the poem, to do several things directly with the image of Gerard, which would speak indirectly of my friend. So, the poem tries to honor them, to understand them, and lastly to bring them out on paper and thus diminish the intensity of the hold they have on me.

In the first stanza of the poem, I tried to show Gerard in perhaps one of his best states, for what, after all, would know more about the sea than a lobster. And his attempt to trace this knowledge back to Spring must, I think, be one of vision. The second stanza was meant to show the city overwhelming him and taking him from his vision to what we would normally call reality. The third stanza should show a return to the "darkness" with the power of vision of the first stanza, which could move him from Paris to Normandie and bring crowds into his empty cell, but without the intense logic he had shown earlier. And finally by leaving Gerard lost in his own mind and thereby my friend smiling through the metal screens of an institution, I can in a sense save myself.

In writing the poem then, I think I have honored the two men in the best and probably the only way I can. This is assuming the poem is a "good" poem, and I am not even sure of that. It has helped me to understand more about who I am, which may or may not lend more understanding of them, and the poem has certainly helped ease the pressure of writing about them. Whether any of the three objectives is met for the reader, I cannot say. But for me they will only continue until the next set of circumstances forces me to try again, through a poem, to meet them.

Raymond Carver

Raymond Carver was born in 1938. He has a B.A. from Humbolt State College in California, and spent a year in the Iowa Writers' Workshop. He has been a janitor, saw mill hand, retail clerk, theatre program seller, delivery man, and editor for a publishing firm. Also a writer of fiction, his stories have appeared in *Esquire, Harper's Bazaar,* and *Best American Short Stories.* His two books of poems are *Near Klamath* (1968), and *Winter Insomnia* (1970), and one of his stories is scheduled to appear in *O'Henry Prize Stories* of 1973. Carver has also won the Wallace Stegner Literary Fellowship for 1973.

WINTER INSOMNIA

The mind would like to get out of here
Onto the snow. It would like to run
With a pack of shaggy animals, all teeth,

Under the moon, across the snow, leaving
No prints or spoor, nothing behind.
The mind is sick tonight.

It wishes Chekov were here to minister
Something—three drops of valerian, a glass
Of rose water—anything, it wouldn't matter.

The mind can't sleep, can only lie awake and
Gorge, and listen to the snow gathering
For the final assault.

DRINKING WHILE DRIVING

It is August.
I have not read a book in six months
except something called *The Retreat From Moscow*
by Caulaincourt.
Nevertheless, I am happy
riding in a car with my brother
and drinking from a pint of Old Crow.
We do not have any place in mind to go
we are just driving.
If I closed my eyes for a minute
I would be lost, yet
I could gladly lie down and sleep forever
beside this road.
My brother nudges me.
Any minute now, something is going to happen.

THE WALL

Drifting outside in a pall of smoke,
I follow a snail's streaked path down
the garden to the garden's stone wall.
Alone at last I squat on my heels, see

what needs to be done, and suddenly
affix myself to the damp stone.
I begin to look around me slowly
and listen, employing

my whole body as the snail
employs its body, relaxed, but alert.
Amazing! Tonight is a milestone
in my life. After tonight,

how can I ever go back to that
other life? I keep my eyes
on the stars, wave to them
with my feelers. I hold on

for hours, just resting.
Still later, grief begins to settle
around my heart in tiny drops.
I remember my father is dead,

and I am going away from this
town soon. Forever.
Goodbye, son, my father says.
Toward morning, I climb down and wander

back into the house. They are still
there, God help them all, waiting,
fright splashed on their faces now,
as they meet my new eyes for the first time.

HUNTER

Half asleep on top this bleak landscape,
Surrounded by chukkers,
I crouch behind a pile of rocks and dream
I embrace my babysitter.
A few inches from my face
Her cool and youthful eyes stare at me from two remaining
Wildflowers. There is a question in those eyes
I cannot answer. Who is to judge these things?
But deep under my winter underwear
My blood stirs.

Suddenly,
Her hand raises in alarm—
The geese are streaming off their river island,
Rising, rising up this gorge.
I move the safety. The body gathers, leans to its work.
Believe in the fingers.
Believe in the nerves.
Believe in THIS.

DESCHUTES RIVER

This sky, for instance:
closed, gray,
but it has stopped snowing
that is something. I am
so cold I cannot bend
my fingers.
Walking down to the river this morning
we surprised a badger
tearing a rabbit.
Badger had a bloody nose,
blood on its snout up to its sharp eyes:
 prowess is not to be confused
 with grace.

Later,
eight mallard ducks fly over
without looking down. On the river
Jack Sandmeyer trolls, trolls
for steelhead. He has fished
this river for years
but February is the best month
he says.
Snarled, mittenless,
I handle a maze of nylon.
Far away,
another man is raising my children,
bedding my wife bedding my wife.

ON "DRINKING WHILE DRIVING"

I'm not a "born" poet. Many of the poems I write I write because I don't always have the time to write fiction, my first love. An offshoot of this interest in fiction is that I'm interested in a story line, and as a result I suppose many of my poems are narrative in bent. I like poems that say something to me the first time around, although poems I like a lot, or don't like especially but can see value in, I'll read a second, third, and fourth time to see what makes them go. In all my poems I'm after a definite mood or ambience. I constantly use the personal pronoun, although many of the poems I write are sheer invention. Very often, however, the poems do have at least a slender base in reality, which is the case with "Drinking While Driving."

The poem was written a couple of years ago. I think it has a certain amount of tension, and I want to believe it's successful in presenting a sense of loss and faint desperation on the part of a narrator who seems—to me anyway—at dangerously loose ends. When I wrote the poem I was working an eight to five job in a more or less decent white collar position. But, as always with a full-time job, there was not enough time to go around. For a while I wasn't writing or reading anything. It was an exaggeration to say "I haven't read a book in six months," but at the time I felt it was not far from the truth. Some while before the poem happened along I had read *The Retreat From Moscow* by Caulaincourt, one of Napoleon's generals, and once or twice during that period I had ridden around at night with my brother in his car, both of us feeling aimless and hemmed in and working on a pint bottle of Old Crow. Anyway, there were these vaguely remembered facts or traces in my head, along with my own very real feelings of frustration at the time, when I sat down to write the poem. I think some of all this came together.

I really can't tell you more about the poem or the process. I don't know how good the poem is, but I think it has merit. I can tell you it's one of my favorites.

Peter Cooley

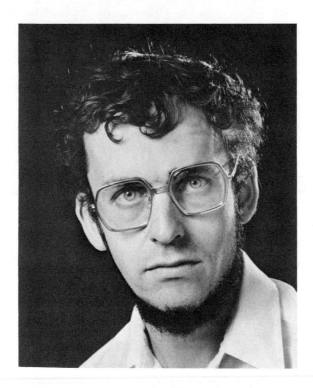

A native of Detroit, Michigan, Peter Cooley was born in 1940. He holds degrees from Shimer College, the University of Chicago, and the University of Iowa. Currently he is teaching at the University of Wisconsin in Green Bay in the College of Creative Communication, and is poetry editor for *North American Review*. His poems have appeared in such magazines as *Poetry Northwest, Denver Quarterly, Kansas Quarterly, Colorado Quarterly*, and *Seneca Review*.

THE MAN WHO CLOSES HIMSELF
after Guillevic

You don't find him in crowds,
the man who closes himself.
He doesn't need hiding
where it's so dark
with the fires, the keys
and the spiral where each step
will never rise.

*　*　*

He has learned to go
through doors nailed shut,
the man who closes himself,
and felt his body sprayed
into the grains of the wood.
He has carried his doors
until he will drop.

*　*　*

He has hands,
he has feet,
he has a head,
it isn't easy
and then the torque of the wind
is never the same
at any minute.

*　*　*

He knows corridors,
the man who closes himself,
and mirrors, the floors
where his face will go on walking
after he's gone.
Mirrors that are reflections
of all his keys.

*　*　*

He wakes
to find himself
in the mouth of the sun
falling
without his moving
into that sun.

*   *   *

He finds himself
in the bark of a tree
where he can hide
with the hollow inside.
All night he will walk
in that tree's circle, unable
to rise through the tree
in the way of the moon.

*   *   *

He has seen his other
watching in doorways,
approaching in smoke,
a light growing closer
under his skin.
For the man who closes himself
the other is skin.

*   *   *

For the man who closes himself
what is the sun?
what are the trees?
what are the zones of the wind?
what would it be
to sow himself
starting from the center.
He knows this much
it's his own way.

*   *   *

For his wife
there is nothing left
except in silence
beyond the words.
In bed she moves
under his hands like water,
water that will not rise
to drown him
but in minutes.

* * *

Even the laughter
of his small daughter
is too loud, too hard
and cannot touch him
going around.

* * *

He would like to get away
from all this, to go
to the edge of the field
where he could lie
with the fireflies
of snow that would come down
to light his eyes.
These eyes that want to go
beyond the edge of the field.

* * *

He wants the light
to go out
in the back of his head,
that has been burning
for so long now.
But he has no words,
the man who closes himself,
to hold that light.

* * *

He would like to walk
in the poem, to talk
in it, to hear the light
lifting his body off
as he spoke his way, the earth,
the water, fire
rising out of his breath.
But the words turn him here.

* * *

There is the spiral,
there are the mirrors,
there is still the wind.
He crosses these, always alone,
the man who closes himself,
wanting to be
with none of these, to be
wherever they take him
to make his way.
The reason he's going
is still
to be made up.

FLOATING COATHANGERS

I hoist the mummy, an armful of frozen plaster,
from its hook in the closet. Dragging it to the desk,
I stretch it out. Now to unspool blue inches of its
feet. The wrapping is ticker-tape in my fingers, it
sticks like a tongue. By the ankles I know it's not
who I want again. I want the face I can make over into
mine, putty of cheeks that take a dent from the thumb,
slaps from the back of a hand.
In the village square the tatooed madonna rocks
on alabaster haunches, nude and pocked with revelation.
Others come to leave their kisses in her skin. They
leave knowing how to love. I never confess.
When night comes, I'll go out to hunt for shadows
I can penetrate with mine. Trees are best, but they move

away in circles with the grip of a foot. They seem to
cringe. I'll walk the wet grass, to feel the ringing
of a voice I've never known, opening in the earth, to
give herself to me, through soles of my shoes.

AH, WILDERNESS

After watching all night from a petrified
side of the mountain for cougars,
jackels and lizards, hyenas, horned toads,
but noticing only a pigeon who left
a wet, threatening note on a stone,
I stumbled down to the desert at dawn
for my breakfast of locusts and wild honey.
While I was hunting up the honey I tried
to think what to tell them later at home.
But just as I saw a bumblebee,
I thought I heard someone over the mountain
calling my name, and I ran
around to the other side to find
a cave like a mouth, yawning and hungry.
Outside I waited for thunder, flood,
the pigeon, even. Finally, I whispered
my name and "Who are you?"
Five minutes later a voice repeated
"Peter," so I went inside
and went to sleep.

THE WHITE ROOM

I wake up in a room that seems to be snowing.
But nothing moves. On a shrill white table a white lamp
prints shadows in the shape of spoons.
  The question had been how to get the cat over
water. I tried every position. All those eyes of the
judges, their pulsing slope, the indefatigable choices
of what would lead me here. And the rim of the sea,
at first a blue sickle, then lifting its locked fingers
at me, then falling back.

There are no windows, no doors, to this room.
Somewhere, in the distance, children are moaning.
The sound is glass keys falling through water, collecting
as they break.
  In the shadow on the table, a pitcher and cup.
I get up, go to them. A black milk. I pour it out,
drink. Now the room begins to sway under my feet,
corners near the ceiling kicking with claws of things that
want to come in. When I look at my hands, I can see
through the stretches of skin. Formations of bones are
clearing to crystal.

ON "THE WHITE ROOM"

Dream? Reality? Poem? Prose? "The White Room" skirts these, not want-
ing to be any one of them unless it can be all. What it came from was a
"real" experience; I had gone to sleep in a room with white walls and
curtains. Somewhere at the end of sleep I found my way to the dream-
room of the poem and when I woke my white circumstance seemed
dream. Awake, I was still as if I were dreaming.

In composition of the poem I have tried to give the atmosphere ap-
propriate qualities for somewhere outside time and space as we usually
know them. These aspects are made up, not remembered. In most of my
poems I find the imaginary has to be injected into the real to make it
come alive for me as a poem.

I wrote the poem several years ago—before prose poems became as
camp as they are now. Then the poem demanded to be written in prose
as a freedom from the stanzas I usually thought in. Now I sense how
stylized "The White Room" seems. If I were to write it today, I would
try for less internal rhyme and more discontinuity.

In this poem I can see some of the obsessions of my other work: Isola-
tionism, Purification, Waking-Dreaming, Birth-Death, Metamorphosis.
I'm aware of these "themes" after the poem has cooled off; but they
have nothing to do with the impetus to write it, of course. That's com-
pulsion, the satisfaction of some appetite nothing else will slake.

What is the prose poem? I hear someone asking. Yes, it's a poem with-
out line breaks. But it can have the richness and density I look for in a
poem and which prose can sustain only with great difficulty and still
soak us in that fuller and wider illusion that seems like fictional life.
The prose poem is a slice of that illusion, but unlike the poem by Poe's
definition, it's not just to be read at one sitting: it's bite-size.

Sam Cornish

Sam Cornish was born in 1935. After spending some time in the United States Army and with an insurance company, he became a writing teacher, and presently is at the Highland School in Roxbury, Massachusetts. He is co-editor of *Chicory* (1969), an anthology of writings from the black ghetto, and co-author of *Your Hand in Mine* (1969), a children's book. His poems have appeared in *Journal of Black Poetry, Massachusetts Review, New American Review,* and other magazines. His first collection of poems, *Generations,* was published by Beacon Press in 1968.

he had a name
and no father
packed his books
in milk crates
never reading them just watching
the colors in the afternoon dust

his clothes were patched jersey
he had nothing to say
but watched the strangers
across the street
listened to the fights upstairs

when he was thirteen
he found the yellow seasons of summer
were dark rooms
where girls undressed for boys
he found love in the smooth face of a girl
that has since become darker
and carried more children than he had freckles

he would come into her cold apartment
wondering if he had the special knowledge
that women wanted from men
endured the pain she moaned
the odor between her breasts

and wanted god to remember
he was young

and in much trouble

with himself

FREDERICK DOUGLASS

my mother twice in her life on worn feet
walked an afternoon against the southern
heat to bring me a ginger cake
her face lined with scars in wrinkled
skin was only twenty three

my mother carried me in the fields and slept
on black ground as i turned within our skin
and as a child white fingers walked into her
mouth to count the teeth and raise the price

i was born somewhere between the shacks
and evenings when shadows were tired across
the fields and dresses gray with dust

GENERATIONS 2

sometimes he walked to occupy
his feet

to lower the sky or identify
trees

arrived at home with dust that survived
in his breath

he never fished but counted scattered
boxcars

the death of jungles and natives
in jelly glasses

blew his breath in battered
paper bags

sailed ship for the new world
in the kitchen sink

when asked about his ambition
he always held

his words

RAY CHARLES

do you
dig ray
charles

when the
blues are
silent

in his throat

& he rolls
up his
sleeves

FORECAST

All will die
watch out for
the man with the soap
and the towels

ON "GENERATIONS 1"

Perhaps for me the poem "Generations 1" starts with the memory of a
grocery store below the apartment where I used to live. There was the
smell of fresh made coffee in the hallways of the house that made me
glad the store was there. The store was still there when I returned to
Baltimore, the Jews that owned it were heavier, their children had

moved away to a college town thinking about the war and the black children they grew up with and never really knew.

We lived and grew up there and now the same windows and houses were holding the same people that were a part of my life. So much had happened that they were unable to talk about. They had lived their lives and kept no records.

"Generations 1" was to be a poem about growing up, being black a long time ago, growing up in a time when you laughed at Amos and Andy, and soul music was something you heard on the radio late at night.

I walked to the east side of Baltimore trying to find and remember the boys that grew up with me and were still living on the streets: laughing, talking and thinking about the streets, the playgrounds that had turned into parking lots, or weeded places after the riots. The poem grew out of those meetings and remembering what it was like to grow up alone, how I felt about women, the church, what I wanted to do with my life. But many of my friends were dead through accidents, the war, drugs, and alcoholism. The people who married lived in the former homes of white-men proud of their club cellars.

The second draft was done after I visited my mother, walked through the rooms in her apartment and touched the books, the pictures, and the dark bookcases of my childhood. Remembered not what I was told by my friends, but recalled that I knew nothing about what had happened in my life. So I had to rewrite to include the life not only of myself but the lives of my friends and the words of mother talking about a son that could not recognize himself as his mother told him about growing up and being a part of the life that was to become the poem "Generations 1."

Tom Crawford

Tom Crawford was born in Flint, Michigan in 1939 and has B.A. and M.A. degrees from Sacramento State College. A former switchman and brakeman on the railroad, Crawford lives in Suisan Valley, California where he teaches at Solano College. His poems have appeared in various magazines including *Chelsea, Quarry, Ironwood,* and *North Stone Review.*

the feeding cycle of the catfish

it is said they feed at night
using their feelers
like fingers
along the muddy bottom
but no one can explain
the sharp barbs
near the mouth
peculiar to this species

in some places
it has been reported
they are attracted to fire
and in other places
they say the large ones
actually crawl out of the rivers
at night
and travel miles
to invade the local farms
eating hogs—
this may be legend . . .

but i know
they can live out of water
for days
and if you pry open one's mouth
you may see a variety of cans
rusty hooks
half eaten bodies
or old men sitting around a campfire
smoking

everything must go

tonight
the moon shines like a new ax
among the dark trees

and i understand that everything must go
when the trees begin to drop their branches
like tired arms
and fall to the ground
before they are even struck
crushing the deer
who wait patiently for the blow
and the birds accept their broken wings
and smother quietly in the branches
i understand
and when the windows explode
against the flying weight of splintered bone
and bodiless wings
that wound me through the covers
and patches of fur fill the room
like flying bats or hands
and when the house begins to move
then stumbles
like a dying bear
because the timbers are caving in
like broken ribs
i don't mind
because now even the moon is falling
and i understand that everything must go

enormous sleep

my growing up
is trying to put old senses to sleep
and making my bed continuously
smaller
but by myself

all night in this room
i think of the boy who once
insisted on sleeping alone
who followed animals down banks
of rivers to drink

who loved the softness of feathers
that held him high in the air
and who hand-fed all starving things
into forgiveness
in this enormous sleep.
yes
now i'll wait for morning

but something has happened
i am uncertain—
the room is smaller
i am smaller
i want to stay in my bed
and wait for night
coming down the hall
like an old nurse carrying the needle

ON "THE FEEDING CYCLE OF THE CATFISH"

To begin with, I'm always looking for a poem. But there is no way I can explain that, really, except to say I can't imagine doing anything else except when I'm fishing. Very often a poem gets started when I find a line somewhere. Maybe the line comes out of my head, a line about a house, after I've been thinking about houses or looking at a photograph of a house. God knows where the damn thing comes from, and it doesn't matter—a billboard, a book I've read, another poet's poem, something someone says to me; the important thing is I love the sound of it, the way it feels in my mouth and the way it sits on the page. To give you an example, a friend of mine, G. Thompson, and I were driving back to Sacramento. A big car rolled past us going like hell with a couple of women in the front. But all I saw were the elaborate bouffants, very dark and slick looking. Then Gary said, "It's ok Tom—they were just a couple of mean looking secretaries heading for Reno." What a marvelous line. I mean not only does the line sound good, (there's no way I could get tired of hearing it) but it suggests all sorts of possibilities as a poem. Coming in just the right place in the poem, that line could drop you. It's possible. Then again, the line may never get into anything. All I know at the time is my head begins to see these kinds of images in terms of a poem.

This is pretty much what happened with the catfish poem. It got started when I began turning the title line over in my head. I don't remember now how the poem came together, though I can assure you it wasn't in a flurry. I do remember that the title (I knew then it had to be the title) determined to a large extent the tone of the poem. It was so instructional and scientific sounding that it seemed natural to play on it in an ironic way; though I must admit that consideration of tone is something I'm more conscious of now than when I wrote the poem. And while the title came pretty easy (D. Schmitz and I were fishing one day in his office), the poem itself was awfully hard to write, taking several days. Not only were there many, many typewritten drafts, to say nothing of all the thought I gave to it in between the actual writing (I even dreamed about it), but the poem refused to develop in any orderly fashion, which is usually the case. As I recall, the top end, the first stanza, was ungodly flat and caused me no end of despair. But at least it got me started. You see, I had no preconceived notions about where the poem was going, nothing beyond a visceral sense of what I wanted to say; that is, I knew it had to be dark. I was fascinated with the idea of catfish eating hogs, however, and that particular thought was in my head (I think I read about it somewhere though probably not in *Scientific American*) long before I had any idea I would write the poem.

Of course, as I look at the poem now, months later, it's tempting to say oh yes, the editorial touches like "it is said . . ." and "it has been reported . . ." and "they say . . ." are all devices I consciously employed to dramatize the last stanza. But it just isn't true. Ideas come later perhaps. "the feeding cycle of the catfish," like any poem I've written, begins with a line that generates certain emotions in me. What I try to do, and this is where the plain hard work comes in, is find images that will bring these emotions to life—to the page. I don't want to make this business sound precious, because it's not (well, maybe a little) but neither is it a business of ideas first. If I actually had a big idea, a scheme so to speak, I would be scared to death, as well as bored, and the poem would never get written. I can look at the catfish poem now and say wow! this is a fine metaphor for talking about poetry or the poet, (the title of the poem is also the title of my book) but this had virtually nothing to do with writing the poem.

Perhaps the only thing I can say that makes sense about this poem or any I've written is I write and I write until the damn thing works. And besides, what does any overgrown catfish have to do with anything?

Philip Dacey

Philip Dacey has published extensively in the "little" magazines as well as in *Esquire* and *The New York Times*. He has also published several pamphlets of poems. Born in 1939, he has taught at Stanford University, the University of Iowa, the University of Missouri at St. Louis, and Miles College. Currently he is Associate Professor of English at Southwest Minnesota State College in Marshall, Minnesota and the editor of the magazine *Crazy Horse*.

THE ANIMALS' CHRISTMAS

They are always living
in Christmas.
Though they walk years
through a field
they can never step

out of the birth of a god.
In each dark brain
a star
sending light through their sinews
leads their hooves

forward from one miracle
to another,
the gleams
tipping grass
like the bright eyes

of uncountable millions
of babies
a field has borne.
When they rub a tree,
a secret myrrh

descends onto their backs.
They carry and offer it
without even trying.
From their nostrils
they breathe good news.

THE PERFECTIONIST

Peter Kubelka, an Austrian filmmaker, has been making films for eighteen years
but his total works run less than forty minutes. *Schwechater*, a film it took two
years to make, lasts one minute.

Nowhere around him
is anything broken,
he is that careful.
His wife sits perfectly
in a corner,

his children are never
wound up to breaking.
The breaths he produces
are tied in ribbons,
fit for gifts.

When he stretches with
sleepiness, his arms extend
inward, away from the china;
when he speaks to friends,
he scratches each word on a stone.

All his life he's been moving
in slow motion up a long
flight of stairs—one step a year.
Nightly, he dreams of
diving into water

and not splashing.
But the nightmare recurs:
he is sailing
in a mistake like a boat
toward the edge of the world.

PORNO LOVE

For Darlene & Mae

You send me a photograph
of you in which your genitals
are not only exposed
but offered close-up to the lens
like a piece of good advice.
I've never met you
though you say,
"We think you're swell."
I appreciate the gesture:
I've been exposing my genitals
in poems for a long time now,
at least when they're good.
So I know you mean nothing obscene
by it. Your squat is humble,
as mine is, even now.
I am writing this poem
naked, up close.
I am writing it with my penis.
No one but you two sisters
will understand
how such a poem is innocent,
how, as with a confidence to a friend,
no shock is intended,
how what we stick in the faces of our loved ones
is our way of saying, I trust you will not
seal me shut
or cut me off, I love you that much.
Surely we will meet with our clothes on,
that is the point.
But when I say, Thanks for the picture, girls,
it's nicely cropped,
and you say, We liked the feel of your poem,
I'll be thinking how certain private parts
made vulnerable
give greatest pleasure
in a consummation
of good will.

THE AMPUTEE SOLDIER

Look at me move
My one, good hand.
I will conjure with it.

I will make
Another hand, as powerful,
And take it for my own.

With that new hand,
I will make signs
In the air. Even I

Shall not understand them.

ON "THE PERFECTIONIST"

I had discovered the epigraph about a year before I wrote the poem and
tucked it away in my notebook, knowing that someday it would yield a
poem. What eventually triggered off the poem I don't remember, al-
though maybe it came at a particularly bad moment for me, when I was
yearning for a little more perfection in my life, so that the poem was, in
part, a self-mocking lesson to myself. A key distinction—which I hope
is apparent—between Kubelka, or any artist like him, and the subject of
the poem is that Kubelka is a perfectionist when it comes to art (a per-
missible obsession, it seems to me; Yvor Winters reminded us that that's
the only place one *can* achieve perfection), whereas the subject of the
poem seeks perfection in his life, and that obsession is worse than folly.
The tone of the poem is ironic: the perfectionist is careful, he makes
sure nothing is broken, but I mean that to suggest he therefore accom-
plishes nothing also, as he is afraid to take the risk; his wife "sits per-
fectly," and the line-break is designed to underline the irony of "per-
fectly," as she's "in a corner," and has thus apparently been trained by
him not to cause any disturbance in his life or in their life together
(clearly implicit, I hope, is the judgment that such peace is bought at
too great a cost); "wound up" is here a pun, as it means "excited" but
can also suggest toys, his children, whose difficult humanity he refuses to
accept; his breaths are neat little productions, "fit for gifts," and that is
ridiculous and sad, as breath is intimately associated with the life-force,
which is neither neat nor little nor precious (in the sense of refined or

overrefined) as a gift might be. There's a progression of sorts in the poem, from domestic life, to social life (friends), to life in general, though I didn't want that progression to be terribly schematic or terribly obvious. A friend of mine pointed out what amounts to a visual or kinetic pun between stanzas four and five: the space between the diving and splashing (or not splashing) is equivalent to the diver's plunge through space. I believe that that fusion of form and content is there at that point in the poem, though I don't know anymore whether I intended it or not. If any reader should have missed the irony of the poem by the time he gets to stanza five, I would hope that that stanza makes it clear to him: the perfectionist fears, in his dream, sailing off the edge of the world, but what the perfectionist always forgets is that the world (life) is round, and you can't fall off it, regardless of how mistake-filled or messy one's life is. Life *shall* have us, without condition. The poem, then, is about a failed life. In the eyes of the subject, of course, his life is probably a success, but to the extent he achieves what he's after—perfection in an imperfect world—he loses touch with that world, the only one he's got. The 5-stanza, 25-line form is one I've used with considerable regularity since I started writing. It's an arbitrary form, but one I enjoy "filling up" and exploiting.

Stephen Dunn

Stephen Dunn was born in New York City in 1939 and educated at Hofstra University, The New School, and Syracuse University, where he took an M.A. in Creative Writing. Presently he teaches at Southwest Minnesota State College in Marshall, Minnesota. His poems have appeared in *The Atlantic Monthly, Poetry, The New Republic, Poetry Northwest,* and *Kayak.* A winner of an American Academy of Poets Award at Syracuse in 1970 and the Florida Poetry Contest in 1972, Dunn has published a pamphlet entitled *5 Impersonations.*

THE LOSS

Even the tips of their fingers
seem to be retreating

their eyes appear ransacked
of what was wide and American

if you had told them
that history is a small circle, that

toward everybody
a line is moving

they would have laughed
they were the kind

who lose their teeth
when a jack-in-the-box

comes out swinging
though now everything is clear, clear

as an old telegram.
Some are sitting by themselves

some have folded their hands
as far removed from prayer

as poker players who have found themselves
with nothing

AT EVERY GAS STATION THERE ARE MECHANICS

Around them my cleanliness stinks.
I smell it. And so do they.
I always want to tell them I used to box,
and change tires, and eat heroes.

It is my hands hanging out
of my sleeves like white gloves.
It is what I've not done, and do not know.
If they mention the differential
I pay whatever price. When
they tell me what's wrong beneath my hood
I nod, and become meek.
If they were to say I could not
have my car back, that it was theirs,
I would say thank you, you must be right.
And then I would walk home,
and create an accident.

BIOGRAPHY IN THE FIRST PERSON

This is not the way I am.
Really, I am much taller in person,
the hairline I conceal reaches back
to my grandfather, and the shyness my wife
will not believe in has always been why
I was bold on first dates. All my uncles
were detectives. My father a crack salesman.
I've saved his pins, the small acclamations
I used to show my friends. And the billyclub
I keep by my bed was his, too; an heirloom.
I am somewhat older than you can tell.
The early deaths have decomposed
behind my eyes, leaving lines apparently caused
from smiling. My voice still reflects the time
I believed in prayer as a way of getting
what I wanted. I am none of my clothes.
My poems are approximately true.
The games I play and how I play them
are the arrows you should follow: they'll take you
to the enormous body of a child. It is not
that simple. At parties I have been known to remove
the kind of book from the bookshelf
that goes best with my beard.
My habits in bed are so perverse they differentiate me

from no one. And I prefer soda, the bubbles just after
it's opened, to anyone who just lies there. Be careful:
I would like to make you believe in me.
When I come home at night after teaching myself
to students, I want to search the phone book
for their numbers, call them, and pick their brains.
Oh, I am much less flamboyant than this.
If you ever meet me, I'll be the one with the lapel
full of carnations.

TO THE UPRIGHT

Excuse me. Do not speak of nerves
gone dead, nor of pain

with no hurt inside it.
Perhaps

men with bad knees
shouldn't be expected

to do deep things, or move
to fix whatever in the world

is wrong. Theirs was a youth
without spring, of endless

drag bunts they dreamed
of beating to first.

So what if their knees stick out
in every conversation.

So the natural crack of bones
as they rise from low chairs

sends them into the hollow
of old trumpets. So what.

You see through them with an eye,
perhaps, that has never turned in

where the water collects
around your heart.

IF I WERE IN CHARGE OF EPIPHANIES

small, significant bumps would appear on your skin
and the accidental laughter in church would begin
to form a pattern, say, in the Dakotas.

Soon you would look to yourself for miracles.
People south of Bismarck would start to wonder
why women come out of supermarkets totally satisfied.

Around your enormous navel
small hairs would spring up and spell words
you were never able to say.
Van Gogh would appear in wheatfields with a basket
of new eyes.

You would come to me with questions.
A young girl in Kansas would swear to her parents
(and later to the world) that an agnostic revealed
himself to her behind a huge rock.

You would feel something turn deep inside you,
like a key.
All the bramble in Northern Texas would be accused
of immolation.

ON "THE LOSS"

I am only occasionally interested in the process by which my poems get
created, though almost always fascinated by other poets' elucidations of
their own process. So I can see some value to what I'm about to do. Still,

there's something counter-productive to knowing too much about your own process, especially for someone like myself who believes in "gifts," in lines that seem to come from nowhere. Yet, to admit to being entirely unselfconscious would be a lie. The interesting questions for me are: How much did one know about his poem before he started it? How much did he discover about it after he finished it? And what decisions did he have to make along the way?

Before beginning "The Loss" remember that I wanted to write a poem about our involvement in Vietnam, but didn't want to write a "war" poem. And I had some lines I liked very much from an old, bad poem that I had been trying to work into the poems I was then writing. They were "If you had told them/ that history is a small circle/ that/ toward everybody/ a line is moving" and "they were the kind/ who lose their teeth/ when a jack-in-the-box/ comes out swinging." These lines seemed particularly appropriate to the themes of loss and folly which I had in mind for the Vietnam poem. This was all I knew about the poem before I began and I think most poets would attest that it was a lot.

All I can say is that the rest of the lines grew out of the lines that preceded them and the beginning came out of the inexplicable. Of course there were the unavoidable "conscious" decisions I had to make, like the choice of couplets, how or if to punctuate, where to break a line. I don't often write in couplets but after some trial and error it seemed to me that this poem was asking for couplets. That is, each grouping of two lines seemed sufficiently strong and coherent to stand by itself. Generally, I think that writing in couplets is a risky business. You draw a lot of attention to the lines when you float them out there like that and if any few of them are weak you're in trouble. Originally I wrote the poem without any divisions between lines (a usual practice of mine) and somewhere along the way decided on couplets.

Punctuation—the poem didn't seem to require any more punctuation than I have included; that is, to be read clearly. One incidental detail that I couldn't resist—the only period in the poem, the only full stop, occurs after the word "telegram." It's my own in-joke. So far only one person who has read the poem has caught it.

About line-breaks, I don't spend a lot of time thinking about where to break a line. You either have a sense of what constitutes a line or you don't. I break a line when it seems like it's over, when it would be vulgar to add one more word to it. That's the rule of thumb I followed in "The Loss."

Finally, I hope the poem is larger than its original intention. If it isn't I probably have failed. I would hope that one should be able to get something from it without ever thinking about Vietnam.

David Allan Evans

David Allan Evans was born in 1940 in Sioux City, Iowa and has degrees from Morningside College and the University of Iowa. His poems have appeared in various publications like *Shenandoah, Poetry Northwest, Kansas Quarterly, The New York Times, Esquire,* and the Borestone *Best Poems of 1969.* He is presently living in Brookings, South Dakota and teaches at South Dakota State University.

POLE VAULTER

The approach to the bar
is everything

unless I have counted
my steps   hit my markers
feel up to it   I refuse
to follow through
I am committed to beginnings
or to nothing

planting the pole
at runway's end
jolts me to my task
out of sprinting
I take off   kicking in
and up   my whole weight
trying the frailty
of fiberglass

never forcing myself
trusting it is right
to be taken to the end
of tension   poised for
the powerful thrust to
fly me beyond expectation

near the peak
I roll my thighs inward
arch my back   clearing
as much of the bar as I can
(knowing the best jump
can be cancelled
by a careless elbow)

and open my hands

THE CATTLE GHOSTS

(Sioux City: I am standing where Armour's used to be)

where they came from once
they come from yet:
a place far off and quieter
for its few swallows
and peeled, face-sunken barns

in the spittled wombs of trucks
through Iowa's screaming nights
they come head on

to this louder land
of the kick and prod
and hammered breath

dying is a shy habit here
that goes on always:
the one with the face of a friend
the one with the mushroomed eye
the one with the limp

I am near them all
though the fifth-floor heavens fall

FORD PICKUP

call me the Valiant heading west on Fourteen into the frozen
Dakota January sun and the one suddenly ahead the red
Custom Ranger with Texas plates and his woman taking
their time and all of my eye as he sits straight and high
beneath a white Stetson nodding politely over frost heave
and she has my long my black my favorite hair with a ribbon
exactly the color of the pickup and feeling the cab's air
and now she scoots his way and lays her head on his shoulder
while he adjusts his hat and sways briefly over the yellow line
so then as they talk her hands are a bird's nest in her lap
to which the knuckles of his loose right hand are always returning

POEM WITHOUT A METAPHOR

for father, dead seven springs

the seventh robin
lights on the thumb
of my son

my lilac bush
is doing its
white explosions

a south breeze
stirs my unnamed tree

the Missouri
swells far from the
bluff of your grave

a Dakota farmer
inverts a corn field

a rock
will soon go skimming
the perfectly round
pond of childhood:

seven springs
and still I lack
the metaphor
of your death

ON "POLE VAULTER"

Whatever its failures may be, this poem has most of those qualities I like
in poems.

First, it has drama. I like dynamic poems, those that move in time and
space. I take Frost seriously when he says that a poem is as good as it is
dramatic. A poem that describes an action has a kind of built-in form: a
beginning, middle, and end. Much of my writing deals with athletes, and

I often use a varied anapest, since for me, the anapest can most nearly approximate the rhythm, energy, and action of sports. I think this may come through in lines like:

> trusting it is right
> to be taken to the end
> of tension   poised for
> the powerful thrust to
> fly me beyond expectation

and:

> near the peak
> I roll my thighs inward

Second, the poem is fairly concise. I dislike flabbiness in poetry. I prefer lines that are spare, clean, tough. The reason has something to do with my belief that there is a Way of saying anything, and only through conciseness (among other things, of course) can that Way be found.

Third, I like the tendency for the poem to say more than it says. That is, the content is not only pole vaulting—though that in itself would be worthy of a poem—but also other activity. Some lines that tend to say more are:

> The approach to the bar
> is everything

and:

> I am committed to beginnings
> or to nothing

and:

> never forcing myself
> trusting it is right
> to be taken to the end
> of tension

Pole vaulting, then, is a metaphor. It allows me to talk about *other* beginnings, *other* situations in which trust is important, and so on. The poem is about vaulting but it is also about sex. A number of years ago I wrote a poem describing a vaulter, which began with words like "the erect pole," and ended with a rather obvious reference to the aftermath of sex. The early poem is bad if only because it is too obvious. Too much is above the surface. But the present poem, I think, is better because it is both direct and indirect. It never actually speaks of anything except the details of pole vaulting; yet the sexual content still probably comes through for the sensitive, experienced reader, especially in phrases like "feel up to it," "planting the pole," "never forcing myself," "powerful thrust," and "near the peak." A good poem, in my opinion, creates an atmosphere which allows effective statements.

("Pole Vaulter" is in one sense strongly autobiographical. One of my gnawing regrets is that I rarely extended myself as an athlete in high school and college. I rarely went all the way. This poem could be the imaginative equivalent of what I *might* have done with a pole in my hand or on the football field.)

Finally, I think the voice of the poem is my own, and therefore right. I always listen for the voice in a poem. I want honesty in that voice, as well as a final modesty, by which I mean an ever-present realization that we triumph and fail at the same time.

Siv Cedering Fox

Siv Cedering Fox was born in 1939 in Sweden, close to the Arctic Circle, and came to the United States when she was fourteen. She now lives in Rye, New York. Her poems have appeared in *The Quarterly Review of Literature, New York Quarterly, Crazy Horse,* and other publications. Some of her work has been translated into Japanese, and she translates to and from Swedish. She has won various awards for her poetry as well as for her photography.

HANDS

I

When I fall asleep
my hands leave me.

They pick up pens
and draw creatures
with five feathers
on each wing.

The creatures multiply.
They say: "We are large
like your father's
hands."

They say: "We have
your mother's
knuckles."

I speak to them:
"If you are hands,
why don't you
touch?"

And the wings beat
the air, clapping.
They fly

high above elbows
and wrists.
They open windows
and leave

rooms.
They perch in treetops
and hide under bushes
biting

their nails. "Hands,"
I call them.
But it is fall

and all creatures
with wings
prepare to fly
South.

II

When I sleep
the shadows of my hands
come to me.

They are softer than feathers
and warm as creatures
who have been close
to the sun.

They say: "We are the giver,"
and tell of oranges
growing on trees.

They say: "We are the vessel,"
and tell of journeys
through water.

They say: "We are the cup."

And I stir in my sleep.
Hands pull triggers
and cut
trees. But

the shadows of my hands
tuck their heads
under wings
waiting
for morning,

when I will wake
braiding

three strands of hair
into one.

ORNITHOLOGY

The woodcock rises
in a complicated dance.
The cardinal has color.
The lark has song.
And some small birds
attract their mates
with intricate
constructions.

I brush my hair,
wear bright colors and
French perfume,
and walk around
my garden,

kick a pebble and
pick a rose,
lift the rose up
to my lips
to feel a petal:
penis skin.

POEM

From what strange country do you come, then?
And do they have horses there?
And swallows?
who slip out of mudbanks and barns
to grow wings in the air.

When I sleep I travel far.

Once I saw the whole sea
run up on shore, and mares
reached me in my sleep
and asked:
Where do you want to go?

If they come again I will say:
Take me to his
country—brook-bed, river-bed,
mountain-meadow—where I can be small,
a pebble, and something large like water, wind,
and sun
will hold me.

ON "HANDS"

I'm sitting in bed writing about the poem "Hands." I should be writing
about sitting in bed. Beds are good places. I am writing with my hands.

I go to the study, turn on the typewriter, use my ten fingers. Are my
hands more valuable than my fingers—I have two hands and ten fingers?
What about the whole and the sum of the parts? My vision of hell rises
before me. I enter. There is no fire. A roomful of critics sit there. I have
to read them. I have to listen to them. One says: "Numbers are signifi-
cant. The author mentions hands seven times in the poem. That is once
more than the hands of her three children." I say: "But, well, the
seventh is for the hand I use to greet people I don't like well enough to
hug, or . . ." Another one says: "Plus the title, 'HANDS,' capitalized,
elevated there, on its own level. Capitalization is very important. In this
language we capitalize God, the names of countries, languages, days,
months. Time is on the level of gods, language lives on the level of days."
What can I say? Whatever I had to say about the poem was in the poem.

If I already have written about hands, I should write about feet. I
have two. They are large. They have bumps on their toes. Their nails
look funny. They like to be barefoot. They only wear shoes when they go
out in the winter. They are familiar with the texture of carpets and
gravel. They like cold marble, in the summer, and to be near a fire or a
warm body, in the winter. Right now they want to go outside. It is almost
May. The flagstones have adopted the sun. The grass is waiting for my
feet. Like Ferdinand, they want to smell the flowers.

Virginia Gilbert

Virginia Gilbert was born in Illinois, received a B.A. from Iowa Wesleyan College, and spent two years in the Iowa Writers' Workshop. Presently she is in Korea working for the Peace Corps. Her poems have been published in such magazines as *Crazy Horse, Sumac,* and *The Back Door.*

LOOKING FOR A PLACE TO BE COMFORTABLE

for Barb and Vicki

I

In the cold static of air,
rayon socks glow when stretched.
Worms of light run quickly
through the rows of thread
from one hand to the next.
Sweaters crack loudly
when taken off, skirts
and pants cling tightly
to the loose ends of human hair.

II

I fear death by
electrocution. I have considered
moving to a different part
of the country, Hawaii perhaps.
But I have heard there are volcanoes
there, the bursting of lava
if one goes too near. Perhaps
I could go to Florida but even there
space ships have been known
to have been shocked by lightning.
In remaining, there is the danger
of one being taken unawares,
at any time, but especially
when sleeping. A person, anyone,
possibly a friend could do it
in bending over beside the bed,
touching the wrist lightly
to wake one up.

III

I have thought it out
carefully. This is my plan.

I shall crawl into the hollow
of your palm; leave behind
all possible clothing, let you
do the moving. Between the folds
of your soft skin, I shall be warm,
shall walk in my sleep.
What more do I need?
In a rain, you will be
my umbrella, black wings
spread softly over me.

FINDING YOU

I

Maybe it was the way
I was awakened this dawn,
a fire pouring out of my wrist,
that made me get up and look for you.
Heaven knows where you have been
or where you go at nights. I can only see
the stars burning up
the soles of your feet.

II

If I could say yes,
yes, I understand. All kinds
of people I know leave their houses
at such odd hours gathering stones,
lumps of earth, small green roots.

I would leash you by your necktie
to my throat if I thought it
would do any good.

III

How can I bring you back, anyhow?
I have cracked my feet, dissected

my tongue, pulled off my skin. I have
punched my way through stacks of hay
tented in fields in the October wind,
pulled at the cattails in the marshlands
behind the river, chopped off the ice
thickening on the trees. You are
never any of these.

IV

Maybe you should know I have moved
the bed next to the window.

V

I hope you realize
I need your terrible
good-byes. It gives me something
to look forward to.

WHAT DOES IT MEAN? THIS HARMONICA

But what does it mean? this harmonica
played down the street
by the skinny boy with buckteeth,
night after night,
and that moon, the same old harvest moon,
ripe like a plum dropping into my hands,
and the smell of honey from behind
Simpson's Art Gallery, threatening me,
night after night. I could say
the walks I take are significant,
that they remind me of another life,
that crazy lie about my having
my mother's eyes. Yet, I could never take
my father naked as she had,
he with whiskey dribbling down
his mouth and side, trying to swallow
his pride, mother bathing him

with insults all the time until they both
broke through the window
and made love on the lawn.

Here are my hands, stuck to the ground,
deep with the weight of this heavy moon,
strong with the sticky smell
of honey on black nights
like these. The skinny boy
plays on. His knobby fingers
crank up and down the instrument
he loves so to pieces that the reeds
fall out and separate into wind
and are carried back to him in the wind,
whole. All is well. This evening,
his humble public sit in the grass
waiting for the piece
to be completed. We are all waiting
for the rising of the moon.

ON "LOOKING FOR A PLACE TO BE COMFORTABLE"

It's not very easy to say how one goes about writing a poem. It is a long
and complicated experience and for each poem written, a different one.
Sometimes, a poet is really hit with that "divine inspiration," when a
deep need inside of the person demands to come out, to make its ap-
pearance. Sometimes, a poem gets written because the poet feels that he
has to write in order to not lose contact with the creative process. There
are other reasons too. When I was going about writing "Looking for a
Place to be Comfortable," it began because I had a poetry group meet-
ing to attend the next night and I still hadn't written anything yet. So,
around midnight, I turned off most of the lights in my room, lit some
candles, and, just in general, tried to block out the real world. After a
while, I remembered an incident from when I was visiting some friends.
It was winter and the air in their apartment was very static and dry.
One night, when I was going to bed and was undressing, I noticed my
socks glowed faintly as I removed them. When I held them in my hand,
they looked normal. Whenever I pulled them, however, I could see little
flashes of light running up and down the socks. I was glad to know that
I wasn't imagining my socks glowing and was so excited that I woke up

my two friends who were already asleep. Well, they got excited about the socks too and we had a lively five minutes or so celebrating the glowing of my socks. Anyhow, I guess the experience stayed with me so that a month later, I used that image in my poem. Actually, when I write, it is pretty much out of intuition (as it probably is with most people). I'm sure that much of this poem reflects a desire on my part to get away from the University of Iowa and, at the same time, my desire to stay. It also reflects my interest in getting closer to life and my fear of doing so. I think this poem and most poems I write gets involved in the real me and in the world as I see and interpret it. I try to write with the intent of being as imaginative as possible without losing emotional impact. Some poems succeed and then, some don't. That is the chance that one has to take. All I can say is that with each poem I write, I try to be as innovative as possible. I hope that some day I can really write the great poem that will speak very deeply to the interior of man. But, if I am incapable of that task, I still find writing just plain enjoyable and that, in itself, is the best reason I know for continuing to write.

Robert Gillespie

Born in Chicago, Illinois in 1938, Robert Gillespie has a B.A. from
Cornell University, and an M.A. and Ph.D. from the University of Iowa.
He has taught at the University of Iowa and Lawrence University, and
is now at Colby College in Waterville, Maine. His work has appeared in
magazines such as *The Beloit Poetry Journal, Colorado State Review,
The Wisconsin Review, Black Swamp Review,* and *Epoch.*

Smaller than molehills their breasts
Urge us both, bold Tenzings
And Hillarys, to imagining
Each of them conquered like Everest
By each of us. Or the eyes
They moon with, eyes that dare just
Because they're there, dare us
To fire at the whites of their thighs.
But we're not warriors.
My Sacajawea and your
Pocahontas prove our war
Parties are simply explorers
Of the dull interior brain,
Taking the lay of the land
That lies so cunning and
Different and always the same
To the shiftless feelers of our lives.
Like the mountain men in their raids
On the beaver, we have to trade
Instead of hides our wives
To learn the feel of losing.
We trap in time and the bait
Is our own skin and our feet
Have snagged in the smugness of our choosing.
We learn to leave small caches
On the grand between, on the portage
Between our oats and our dotage,
Hung high enough from our clutches
To keep the mysterious bawdy
That love is: the moon in her place
Reclining with a different face
And never a different body.
We learn to choose our moods
From the girls that lie enisled
Like a unicorn and as wild
In the heart's lost latitudes
As love. Here, a man outlives
His extremes: when we retreat

It's to the suburbs of the heart,
To our old way everyday wives
That we love a little more
For boredom; for proving it
With feeling our girls prove even yet
More continent than we are.

SHAWANO LAKE, WISCONSIN

I have a desk job.
Tilting back in my chair,
feet up, I'm off
to work for myself.
Maintainance man picking up
the boy on a sweet potato
sound of a barred
owl in a white pine,
overseer between two boots
of the whisking morning
steam gives the lake,
sweeping the skylight clear:
at night the nightwatchman.
No vacations.
The pay is good,
a big job that takes an awful
lot of responsibility.
I do everything
down to the pencils.
I have to watch my language.

SNOW WHITE

She found herself 7 no less
dwarfs!
Such disney images—where did they come from, the yellow pages?—
grumpy sleepy sneezy happy dopey doc
Doc?

So why didn't she ever have any little dwarfs?
She was afraid of her father's handlebar moustache?
Who does she think she is, no hostility like the rest of us
toward stepmother? Her mother for dying?
What is really going on out there in that house in the woods?
Do they really know?
Does it ever get dirty and dull
fishy-stale in her innocent linens?
What are their little penises like, Snow White?
Does one finger
one lap another hump?
Does one sneeze? Unnatural
this absence of the natural. This division.
7 safe little men to father Mommy.
Why are they stay at homes?
Does she do the wash and cook casseroles or just be beautiful?
What was she *doing* out there in the wilderness in the first place,
looking for dwarfs?
Who made Snow White her big bed and cookies
letting her sit there and eat?
Home from their gold mine the swarthy dwarfs she inspires bring
bacon and mayonnaise. With love. They make spring
look like a dwarf.
Oh that lovely garden of a girl,
they stay because she takes their seed, because a garden stays.
 They grow. Get roots down. Better men for it.
(And the apple woman and her uxorious
sidekick, what the fuck what a drag why not be the most beautiful
move on freak out kick *free,*
kicked out)
nibble nibble pick pick at the core of civilization
arch-fear proto-hate ur-guilt
their balls fall off like ripe peaches
pussy snow
beautiful sweet and kind and good.
Everybody agrees.
You soak me up, I'll cut you down;
because they soak her up. Because
they *like* it. Like looking up the blood-red and ebony snow
white they wish they came from.

Save us from our littleness
our ugliness without any beautiful touches
oh lift us up.
Now she is home, a king's son's wife, she is fairy tail
she eats roast beef with crackers
listening to the birds chirp
watching the snow melt
wondering where the brave woodcutter
where the men on white horse

ON "SNOW WHITE"

I've been aiming away from the argument-poem that produces, inevitably, the syntax and logic of prose; which inevitably produce argument rather than a sequence of images. To get from the easy assumption that the only valid representation of any thing is a syntactical structure, I'm after a poem that doesn't look sweated and stitched on, a voice talking offhandedly *to* somebody I have in mind who listens, a mind moving rapidly over and under its subject making images that surprise. The kind of conversation that doesn't know how entertaining or revealing it is, what you get in dramatic monologues. Doing short-line poems—sometimes just a word a line—because I was tired of thinking about poems, of propositions about things and not enough of the things themselves (you don't get the dramatic object, you only get yourself or a statement) I was trying for what many people are after—fragments that are wedges of the whole but not necessarily next to one another, trying to get accented syllables off the metrical beat to make the rhythm itself rather than a meter the basic pattern, trying to get line breaks to make irony coax the statement into an argument with itself, to face up to the self-contradictions of the speaker (I'm partial to dramatic monologues for that), trying to get clichés lively. Short lines got more artificial and cute, so the poem that turned out to be "Snow White" came pretty much straight off from thinking about it both as a subject and as a chance to work on these effects in longer (metrically, appearance, self-contained image the length of the line) lines.

The look I like is a combination of innocence, buffoonery, and earnestness. Absurd writing doesn't wrench anything out of shape; it presents it as we sense it. If a piece is funny as a result of deviation from a norm, the norm it deviates from is a literary one more than any reality, and the verbal devices of absurdity amount to contemporary realism. Because fairy tales are so archetypally right for this, often so unaware of their implications, and because there is a ready-made plot, the problem is one of attitude: the facts are there, what you have to do is see them slantwise to put it straight, spoofing the familiar myth to get it back from romance. Get the earnestness from the characters and situations—keep in all the tale's characters and make them do the job of making the point. Begin with something simple, or verifiable, or simply foolish and only after a few lines sidle into discovery and sneak up in earnest. Statement is all right so long as it's undercut, anticipating the opposition so to speak. Explicit symbols are all right too, if there are unexplicit ones. Quick changes in tone, from the absurd to the lyrical, can make the poem a pointy thing without making a direct statement. The poem can't stand still. At the end it has to take off—the soar that lyrics have—it has to contain perplexity without solving itself. It has to keep flying and not come down but stay out there like the myth, a mystery that is always happening.

Elton Glaser

Born in 1945 in New Orleans, Elton Glaser has B.A. and M.A. degrees from Louisiana State University and an M.F.A. with honors from the University of California at Irvine. His poems have appeared in *Poetry Northwest, New York Quarterly, College English, Iowa Review* as well as in many other publications.

MEAL PIECE

Remember always to eat with both eyes open
keeping one eye steadfastly on the meat
which if you let it would rise
without permission and walk off the table
never under any circumstances to return

THE GENERAL'S WIFE

Across the dinner table from me
over the mock turtle, the blind side of the flounder
she explains to us in great detail
the many ways they have
of killing our crewcut boys in combat.

At night all her stars
are hung neatly in the closet.
And sometimes when she stands alone on the balcony
the moon lights up her helmet of hair
with the sheen of burned bodies.

ASIDES AND MEMORANDA

Basket-weavers ravel the Republic.
The annual rainfall is less than one inch.
We learn nothing from the animals.

Here the desks hunker vast as landing fields
upholding, blank beyond experience, the pages
bound and released as official records.

The five-sided saga flashes deadpan on the screen.
Laughter creeps from under the pillows.
We love each other during station breaks.

Of all fish, only the shark has eyelids.
Bodies, black with newsprint, are discovered in the underbrush.
We do not think it is anyone we know.

THE SACRED HEART OF JESUS BLEEDS FOR YOU

No this time it is not the Avon Lady
torturing your doorbell with her perfectly
manicured finger until your eardrums
rattle like loose rivets and the head of
your penis goes numb nope not her this time
at all nevertheless you straighten your tie
and practice a smile in the mirror before
easing open the door and yes there
he is as you've always known he would
be the diaper the long hair and that
lily blooming from his side right
below the heart exposed exactly like the one
on the third overlay under HUMAN BODY, THE
in your revised edition of the *World Book Encyclopedia*
except for three red tears poised on the point of
falling but never falling and you ask him
in as you knew one day you would have to
but no he doesn't care for anything to
drink though you might if you like shove your hand
in that healing wound and your eardrums rattle

ON "ASIDES AND MEMORANDA"

I chose to comment on "Asides and Memoranda" because I think it is
indicative of the work I've been doing in the past year and the direction
in which I am heading. The poems I enjoy writing most all tend to-
wards abstract poetry, a poetry in which language operates for its own
ends. Some of that concern shows itself in "Asides and Memoranda."

If you understand the title correctly, "Asides and Memoranda" is not
obscure, merely oblique. The poem is then a collection of notes and off-
hand comments on a situation; in this case, something like the moral

bankruptcy of the American people caused by their witnessing through various media the moral bankruptcy of the American government, a subject too true and too trite to be faced fully head-on. But I don't want to monomaniacally insist on an interpretation that rigid or pompous. In fact, it bores me to talk about meaning in a poem. Until I had to write this commentary, I had never given much thought to what my poem *meant*. When all the different pieces seemed to hang together as a unit, I felt the poem was finished.

What does interest me is the process of composition. I put together "Asides and Memoranda" from fragments in my notebook. Like most writers, I collect words, phrases, scraps of speech. Then I rummage through my lists, letting chance juxtapositions suggest lines to me. As an example of this kind of "inspiration," consider the line "Bodies, black with newsprint, are discovered in the underbrush." The words "newsprint" and "underbrush" were scribbled near each other in my notebook, and I saw how I could use them in the context of this poem. Once I had enough material pieced together to see where I had to go with the poem, it became only a matter of maintaining the tone and basic premise. Any skill involved concerns what I admitted to the poem and what I expelled, the precise phrasing of lines and their arrangement on the page.

So I do adhere to the notion that poetry is a game, a game of words at play. And studying under Don Justice, who now composes poems with a mixed method of chance and skill, reinforced my "game" approach. Even more importantly, Justice showed me that poetry is a game worth winning: hopefully, the right combination of words will somehow, in a way I don't yet completely understand, make something significant and exciting of a poem.

Most of my excitement in writing "Asides and Memoranda" came from watching how my scraps became transformed into a poem. Lines come from strange places and often change in the context of the whole work. For instance, I had read somewhere that the trouble with young poets today was their willingness to let facts do the work of imagination in a poem, facts such as sharks being the only fish to have eyelids. I don't know whether the author was presenting a true "fact" as his example or just making up one to serve his argument; but I do know I thought it unusual and apt enough to include in "Asides and Memoranda."

Another example: when I originally noted "We learn nothing from the animals," I meant it to approvingly imply that animals have nothing to teach man. But in the poem it takes on a different meaning: man is too self-centered to take lessons from nature. I don't really believe that second meaning, but I think it becomes a valid statement in the poem.

I was also anxious to marshall a series of words that could borrow from and lend to each other. Take the line "The five-sided saga flashes deadpan on the screen." Basically it describes the flat presentation of our Indochina war on the nightly newscast. But I wanted the line to be loaded like a Contac cold capsule: some of it should work immediately, some of it will take longer to make itself felt. If the words do reverberate correctly, it should be a rich line. "Five-sided saga" then becomes not only the Pentagon's southeast Asian *Iliad*, but also brings to mind the continuing melodrama of television soap operas. "Flashes deadpan" re-arranges itself to spell out "Dead" and "flash in the pan." "Screen" becomes a barrier between illusion and reality, not simply a television picture tube. It may be asking too much of the reader to make these jumps and connections, but I think if the surface is intriguing enough, the reader will want to explore deeper and imaginatively experiment with the text.

So I keep writing because language continually amazes me. I take great delight in the fact that "pages" can be both "bound and released." Or, from a line in another poem, that "listen" and "silent" both use exactly the same letters. It sounds too silly to say, but that has never seemed to stop me before: these "quirks" of language seem magical to me, obscure clues to what we are doing here, breathing but bewildered. And if that conviction makes me a hopeless romantic, I accept the charge. With luck and work, it may also make me a poet.

Louise Glück

Born in New York City in 1943, Louise Glück grew up in Long Island, attended Sarah Lawrence College briefly, then Columbia University. She has taught at Goddard College, and is currently teaching at the University of North Carolina in Greensboro. She has won a Rockefeller Foundation grant, a National Endowment of the Arts grant, and the Eunice Tietjens Memorial Prize from *Poetry*. Her poems have appeared widely in magazines and anthologies. Her first book of poems, *Firstborn*, was published in 1968.

THE SHAD-BLOW TREE

—for Tom

I. The Tree

It is all here,
Luminous water, the imprinted sapling
Matched, branch by branch,
To the lengthened
Tree in the lens, as it was
Against the green, poisoned landscape.

II. The Latent Image

One year he focused on a tree
Until, through sunlight pure as never afterward, he saw
The season, early spring, work upon those limbs
Its lasting magic, which the eye
Retains: deep in the brain
The shad-blow coins its leaf in this context,
Among monuments, continuous with such frozen forms
As have become the trained vine,
Root, rock, and all things perishing.

THE FORTRESS

There is nothing now. To learn
The lesson past disease
Was easier. In God's hotel I saw
My name and number stapled to a vein
As Marcy funnelled its corrective air
Toward Placid. I can breathe
Again. I watch the mountain under
Siege by ice give way to blocks of dungeons,
Ovens manned by wives. I understand.
They coil their hair, they turn their
Music on as, humming to herself, the night-

nurse smoothes her uniform. This is
The proper pain. The lights are out. Love
Forms in the human body.

GRETEL IN DARKNESS

This is the world we wanted. All who would have seen us dead
Are dead. I hear the witch's cry
Break in the moonlight through a sheet of sugar: God rewards.
Her tongue shrivels into gas. . . .
                                        Now, far from women's arms
And memory of women, in our father's hut
We sleep, are never hungry.
Why do I not forget?
My father bars the door, bars harm
From this house, and it is years.

No one remembers. Even you, my brother,
Summer afternoons you look at me as though you meant
To leave, as though it never happened. But I killed for you.
I see armed firs, the spires of that gleaming kiln come back, come back—

Nights I turn to you to hold me but you are not there.
Am I alone? Spies
Hiss in the stillness, Hansel we are there still, and it is real, real,
That black forest, and the fire in earnest.

THE UNDERTAKING

The darkness lifts, imagine, in your lifetime.
There you are—cased in clean bark you drift
Through weaving rushes, fields flooded with cotton.
You are free. The river films with lilies,
Shrubs appear, shoots thicken into palm. And now
All fear gives way: the light
Looks after you, you feel the waves' goodwill

As arms widen over the water; Love,

The key is turned. Extend yourself.
It is the Nile, the sun is shining,
Everywhere you turn is luck.

ON "GRETEL IN DARKNESS"

I do not much like talking about my poems. If the poem does not embody the paraphrase, the poem has failed.

"Gretel in Darkness" took shape in a way not usual for me. The first sentence and the latter part of the last (from "it is real. . . .") were its beginning: somehow the one affixed itself to the other. I recognized the two as the start and finish of a poem; I worked from both ends toward the middle. The lines mentioned came up whole, separated themselves as units from the language.

During this period I was reading what we call children's stories. It became clear that the poem I had begun was to be spoken by Gretel, that it was to deal, as does the story itself, with ritual murder.

At the outset the poem contained considerably more of the myth's detail: trailed breadcrumbs, etc. These seemed to diminish the mystery of the poem, to work against what I hoped to make: a poem that stood firmly apart from the story.

The Gretel of the poem dreamed of a world from which all the women she knew were eliminated: the dream realized provides the context of the poem. The speaker finds that she has called into being a world into which she cannot fit. She exists somewhere off to the side, her loneliness rooted in others' refusal to corroborate the substance of her memories. The facts, perhaps. The meaning, no.

To Hansel the escape from the forest was a means to an end: a future. To Gretel the escape is an end in itself. No moment in the ordinary existence she made possible by killing the witch and rescuing her brother can touch for her the moment of the escape. That moment was her triumph; it provided Gretel with an opportunity to experience herself as powerful. The whole episode, the drama in the forest, remains for her charged and present. It is in that episode that she wishes to imbed herself. Unfortunately she is alone in this desire. Their adventure grows increasingly remote to Hansel, presumably because the new life answers his needs. The Gretel of the poem perceives and passionately wishes to alter, the discrepancy between her investment in the forest and Hansel's.

I do not mean to suggest that these concepts preceded the poem. The poem was not constructed cerebrally; it was waited for, over a period of many months.

My obsessive concern at the time the poem was written (two years ago), and before, and since, was abandonment. Undoubtedly someone else would have been preoccupied with other of the undercurrents in "Hansel and Gretel" than those to which I was vulnerable.

Albert Goldbarth

Albert Goldbarth, born in 1948, teaches poetry and creative writing at Central YMCA Community College in his hometown, Chicago. He has an M.F.A. from, as he calls it, "that warped but bright buckle on the nation's Corn Belt, The University of Iowa Writers' Workshop." Goldbarth is a prolific writer whose poems have appeared in such publications as *Poetry, Massachusetts Review, Poetry Northwest, Field* and *Antioch Review.*

FROM THE BRIDGE

I

Exactitude: to memorize
—before it changes
shape—the shape
of moonlight on water.

II

To sink
unclothed through the dark
cold water.
To surface,
into a collar of moonlight.
It glows on the shoulders
and drips down the breast
gold baubles.
The secret of wearing water.
To walk home
among the unlit windows
feeling it flow
from your back like a cape.

III

The gift to proffer
brides and widows:
moonlight
from the rivertop.
To peel it off,
to dig the fingers
under and lift.
You do not fold it.

IV

After digging:
rims of dirt

under the nails
radiate a breath
thin sheen of lunar
light. It is always dusk there.
You name those ten
unexcavated hills where half
moons are rising forever.

V

Conceptualize:
moonlight on water.
Roots will not grow down from it.
A bird will not land on it.
A fish cannot shatter it.
The deer will drink only up to its edges.
They know they were never meant to drink in
moonlight on water.

SURVIVAL

This is the church of giraffes
dying on their knees, who cannot cry out
the length of their pain but must

topple silently, silently
as haunches unconnected to throats
attract carnivores, voiceless as offal.

This is the word they would say,
that rabbits begin with soft twitching
lips ceaselessly, but never finish

until their deaths; when the life
long stuttering of fragile and hesitant
f's: fulfills itself, once, unheard.

This is where we will marry, here
where the teat of the female buffalo hangs
its appendix weight; a hide-away

bed, safe in the walls, where I can love you
finally. Easily hovering overhead, cherubim
cannot appreciate the floorbound blessings

penguins offer: pumping, pumping vestigial
gestures for centuries, their strain inspires
one sublime squawk, long extinct from our language,

and keeps them warm till morning.

BODY MECHANICS

The hand: spread against the cloudless night, stars disappearing and re-
appearing among the fingers' quadrants; this is called the astrolabe,
you can take it from your pocket and unfold it at arm's length; the suns
collect in your palm, perhaps it's the gravity of your five pink half-
moons; you wonder, are they rising? or setting? and sight the stars to
chart direction, to see where you're going, eventually; where every
body's going.

The eye: is pure acceptance; as if at the rim of the Disk Of Light, sun
has been collected here, 93,000,000 miles away; and immersed, and
broken inside the head with an infinite gentleness nothing else inside
the head will ever break with; this is called the prism, you can open its
lid and nothing lies; everything is its color; the joy of a summer after-
noon's spectrum is known to you; we only forget the closing of eyes,
and illuminations preceding sleep; the subtle lustre of ultraviolet, fad-
ing from an eyelash.

The body: in all of its organs, yours; temporal, opaque, delightful; that
is, full of delight; and delight, defined as light-influenced; and influ-
ence in its original usage, that flow of ethereal powers between celestial
bodies affecting ours; as in the park, we are deftly handling love be-
neath this June's entire moon, and we are hand in hand; as in the

park, under August sun strokes, cops eyeing protestors, two separate visions, faced in a blind spot, eye to eye; we are doing, we are here to do; the body, and the body in activity is casting shadows, each body to its own extent; this is called the gnomon; it is this long, there is this much time.

ON SUNDAY, THE BEGINNING OF THE WEEK,
I MAKE A RELIGION

Having stood before the upraised wing of the male fruit fly
vibrating that one song three-thousandths of a second long
that precedes the rite of insect mating:
there is a silence so deep it is singing.
Having heard that sound; having stood before
snow filling a footprint, and hearing its sound,
having counted time by a unit of snowflakes;
having burned my hand, having known the calm
endurance of pain that is a blue island in the yellow
spasms, something to depend on
so hard you leave teeth-marks; having felt wind
against my cheeks like the sonic boom of a moth gone by in darkness,
or perhaps it is the wind of a priest's or a rabbi's
blessing come half-way around the world
like the touch of the breath of a beautiful woman
who mistakes me for her lover; having filled my cheeks
with her wind; having filled my cheeks with my wind
and spumed, a celebrating sperm
whale; having loved, having slept,
having stood before,

There is a silence so deep it is singing.
There is a knowledge of pain so profound it is bliss.
There is a stillness so intense it is a pyrrhic-dance.
There is a distress so sweet it is succour.
There is a sun.
There is a moon.
There is a space so empty, anything
Is possible, it reads like a poem.

112   *Albert Goldbarth*

It is already here.
It is always arriving.

ON "ON SUNDAY, THE BEGINNING OF THE WEEK, I MAKE A RELIGION"

Now it's dim in The Mill, and noisy with clinking, and our steins are half-empty, and Gerry tells me exactly how far down in the dumps a man can be when his woman is off in Ottumwa, Iowa and open to the world. And ol' Al has to order another round, so says the role, and offer advice. And I did, and though it was b.s. then, I think now I'd never cash in that chip, but would pin it instead as a badge on my life: that the man who locks his wife in a chastity belt can never have the privilege of saying Yes, I believe in her; that faith must, by its very nature, always have a bright string of doubt laced up its spine; that true religions are thereby based on illogic and the unprovable, virgin births, splitting seas, future lives, impossibilities; and that this never denigrates faith, but instills faith-given-despite-such-illogic with the strength of the flexing heart. "On Sunday" was written before my deep brief friendship with Gerry began, but I hope is partly-explained by our beer talk: the power of this poem's convictions incorporating and illuminating any of the paradoxical in it, and giving reason to the irrational process of its being written. Merely that I read in a scientific journal of the awesome unknown musical mating ritual of the fruit fly; that it seemed holy; and that, written down in four lines, it prompted a further listing and interpretation of the holy. I wanted a basic holiness, a total holiness, so that even those experiences which, in a limited human view, were painful, became sustenance in a microworld or macrocosmos. There are such visions. The loose chant-like structure enabled me to use ideas, words, phrase-groupings hoarded for months, and encouraged spontaneous creation of intertwining detail. Don't remember for sure, but doubt if the poem took over 1–2 hours. That includes some reworking: "spastic / red-orange" became "yellow / spasms"; "breathed" became "spumed," which led to the inclusion of the fruit fly's mass-opposite; the whale, "a beautiful woman," became modified by "the touch of the breath of," etc. The title came last: I did not consciously set out to reflect/request a religious experience; only in retrospect did the idea of formal, traditional religious categorization rise from the body of the poem to the title-line at the top of the page (as opposed to "Body Mechanics," whose dependence on the awe of natural processes and capabilities is as great, but whose goals and structure—step by step delineation of body parts as mechanisms—came with the title at the head of a blank page). Comparison may be beside the point. But "On Sunday" is not necessarily representative of my work, or of my way of working. Its sense of acceptance perhaps makes it quite akin to the inexplicable wonder of "From The Bridge" and (although the Church of Giraffes is no less efficacious a location for epiphany) sets it in some ways apart from the more rational working-out-of-imagery and more bittersweet consolation of "Survival." For me, at least. At the moment.

Michael S. Harper

Michael Harper was born in 1938 in Brooklyn, New York and moved to Los Angeles in 1951, where he attended college. After a year in the Iowa Writers' Workshop, Mr. Harper taught at various colleges and universities, and currently is at Brown University in Providence, Rhode Island. His books are *Dear John, Dear Coltrane* (1970) and *History is Your Own Heartbeat* (1971), and several other collections are forthcoming. In 1972 he received a creative writing award from the American Academy of Arts and Letters.

BREADED MEAT, BREADED HANDS

The heat of the oven
glazed on the windowed
doors, the percolated lines
of water drizzle down;
she cooks over the heated
fires in a blaze of meat.

The shelled pan-baked peanuts
ground to a paste
pass over the chicken
ripped off by tornadoes.

Raisins of my son's eyes
garnish the pork loin,
kidneys and beef heart.

In the corner the rock salt
and the crushed snow
churn the coconut
ice cream, vanilla
beans and two half-pints
of cream atop the thundering
washing machine.

Boards thick with sweet potatoes,
the pie crust cooled in the icebox,
dough souring on the stovetop,
the hands of our children
damp with flour and butter
of their burning skins,
and the marks of cooking,
churnings of the heated kitchen.

Yogurt to cover the cucumbers,
sauteed onions, the curd of some
cabbaged blood wine, bottled
vinegar which tastes like olive oil.

At the hearth of this house,
my woman, cutting the bits of guile,
the herbs of warmth she has butchered
into the pots,
the pans of grease
that feed this room, and our children,
condensed in the opaque room—
the hearth of this house
is this woman, the strength of the bread
in her hands, the meat in her marrow
and of her blood.

DEAR JOHN, DEAR COLTRANE

    a love supreme, a love supreme
    a love supreme, a love supreme

Sex fingers toes
in the marketplace
near your father's church
in Hamlet, North Carolina—
witness to this love
in this calm fallow
of these minds,
there is no substitute for pain:
seed burned out,
you tuck the roots in the earth,
turn back, and move
by river through the swamps,
singing: *a love supreme, a love supreme;*
what does it all mean?
Loss, so great each black
woman expects your failure
in mute change, the seed gone.
You plod up into the electric city—
your song now crystal and
the blues. You pick up the horn
with some will and blow
into the freezing night:
a love supreme, a love supreme—

Dawn comes and you cook
up the thick sin 'tween
impotence and death, fuel
the tenor sax cannibal
heart, genitals and sweat
that makes you clean—
a love supreme, a love supreme—

Why you so black?
cause I am
Why you so funky?
cause I am
Why you so black?
cause I am
Why you so sweet?
cause I am
Why you so black?
cause I am
a love supreme, a love supreme:

So sick
you couldn't play *Naima,*
so flat we ached
for song you'd concealed
with your own blood,
your diseased liver gave
out its purity,
the inflated heart
pumps out, the tenor kiss,
tenor love:
a love supreme, a love supreme—
a love supreme, a love supreme—

THE BLACK ANGEL

Childhood games,
played without innocence,
and in place of the angel,
take me to a grove of pepper trees;
they lighten my head.

Trees emit their odors,
a natural oxygen tent;
have you noticed the air is heavy
in trees that shed their leaves
without hesitance,
and flow with sap,
and are closest
to the angel's skin;
the eyes, each singly
wide, smarting, unreadable
as the sap, and which
recount the games,
verses, puzzles of other men:
I am reading poems
to this black angel.
Kindled in the shrill
eloquence of other men,
the angel forces open my hands
and in the palms
leaves her footprints.

ON "DEAR JOHN, DEAR COLTRANE"

"Dear John, Dear Coltrane" was written several years before John Coltrane died. Its aim is the redemptive nature of black experience in terms of the painful private life of a black musician. Coltrane's music should be seen as a progression from the personal, in terms of his evolving style, to incantation and prophesy. It is a fusing of tenderness, pain, and power: their melding and fusing at once an internal and external journey/passage: to live with integrity means *to live*; its anthem—"there is no substitute for pain."

Black musicians have always melded the private and historical into the aesthetics of human speech and music, the blues and jazz. The blues and jazz are the finest extensions of a bedrock of the testamental process. Blacks have been witnesses and victims in America. They have paid their dues in external, historical terms.

The poem is therefore a declaration of tenderness, and a reminder to the reader of a suffering beyond the personal and historical to the cultural, that there can be no reservations fixed to sensibility, that personality gives power through the synthesis of personal history and the overtones of America by contact. The poem begins with a catalogue of sexual trophies for whites, a lesson to blacks not to assert their manhood, and that black men are suspect because they are potent. The mingling of trophy and christian vision, Coltrane's minister-father, indicates an emphasis on physical facts—*that there is no refinement beyond the body*—that joy comes from contact, as does pain, in the context of the physical. The antiphonal, call-response/retort stanza simulates the black church, and gives the answer of renewal to any question raised—*"cause I am."*

It is Coltrane himself who chants, in life, *"a love supreme"*; jazz and the blues, as openended forms, cannot be programmatic or abstract, but *modal.* The modality is Coltrane's personality, his various styles, and the residual bedrock of black communal ancestral roots, in and out of the black church, in contact, in America.

Phillip Hey

Phillip Hey was born in Dixon, Illinois in 1942, educated at the University of Wisconsin and the University of Iowa, and is presently living in Sioux City, Iowa, where he teaches at Briar Cliff College. He has published poems in periodicals such as *Field, Hearse, Shenandoah*, as well as in Paul Carroll's anthology, *The Young American Poets*.

Old John is foolish,
and his daughter is beautiful.

* * *

In youth he became famous for wisdom
with money. Now safe beyond need, and too old
to eat well, he builds monuments to himself.

* * *

The wind has changed;
there is some ill about it.
I shall go without sleep.

* * *

If a man choose his women well,
his comrades, his arms—
ah, but you know that one.

* * *

At the prime of age, he took
a great stone and cast it into the sea,
a strong man! And for the poor,
they have their way, he says,
they live or die as befits them.
As well say he cast down his heart.

* * *

As I sing and play my wild instrument.

* * *

I did not go to that city,
drinking while wiser men slept.
You never saw me there.

* * *

Presidents, kings, all you who hold
dominion over the earth and dark sea
with arms and the threat of arms,
if you have breath answer me now:
what is it of peace that you so fear?

* * *

This army, vast and of great strength,
who brought it around to my door?

* * *

These are the bones
of an evil bird, who ate flesh.
How brightly they shine!

* * *

So long as you ask, and so consign
to me your time and disposition,
I answer in kind: bring me
that light where last the moonbeams fell

* * *

We are not here
to wait for dawn.
Now kiss me.

* * *

As they hid from Death, the Many-eyed,
It came upon them, and saw them plain.

* * *

Nor so beautiful as she, with her long hair,
when the wind plays about it, nor so evil.

* * *

These are good days. Here is wine
in plenty, and I sleep each night
with a woman, my wife.

A THANK YOU POEM FOR THE ANDERSONS

I have just been to the Milo
Anderson farm near Willis Nebraska
and it's a fine farm   the worn boards
of the barn   and the gate you lift up
and latch and wire shut (why a man
would be a fool to buy a new gate,
to believe a new gate would work
any better than the old)

this is where we used to milk, Patsy said
and over here you see the new boards, where
the fire started and we fought it out
there wasn't too much damage
you can't burn a farm

some things endure   the earth
in its full measure of a man
bearing the season   his feet rooted
his eyes moving along the hills
as subtle, gentle, loving as a wife
it is the man   the wisdom of his eyes

thank you   as I drive back
to Sioux City, good melons and apples
in my car   pale dust on my shoes
my lungs full with good air

I am taking back my life

here's a man knows what he's going to shoot
knows how knows when   and a little bit why
you better get it right, it's a fortyfour
it knocks a man down like a sharp ax

now he moves easy down the empty street
now stops, feeling the wind a little,
testing; watching the shadows; watching
that other man as he moves;
draws up; stands alone, and tall

it explodes the heart
the horses shy, the music takes up

ON "EPIGRAMS"

I feel odd writing a commentary to any of my recent poems, since if they succeed, they do so because they are self-explanatory. Maybe it would help to comment on how the poem came about.

I try to use a clear and simple language, but one which is also formal, and somewhat alien to the sentence sense of English. I would hope the alienness of this poem's language shows in the long appositive clause, which is more an act of formal address than an addition to the meaning. I want a feeling of deliberateness.

Though the epigram might appear preplanned, the meaning came out much more naturally. I had thought for years that resistance to change is caused by *fear* rather than the desire to preserve the already good; thus the last line, I think a "natural," and everything else followed. "Presidents:" an ugly, modern word, graceless and (according to the last and present ones) dishonorable. "Dominion": an outright lie. Direct address to God in Latin is *Domine*, who is Lord in the right sense, by love and not arms. "Arms and the threat of arms:" is there not at least some suspicion that that's all they have? Thus the repetitiveness of the line, in its monomania as absurd and criminal as MacNamara's speeches. "Breath:" great word almost anywhere; "breath of life, anima, etc;" but also another way. I'm uncomfortably sure that Richard Nixon is a tape-recorder; so is Mao; Brezhnev; most of them. Real men don't take in God's air for the purpose of killing or reviling. Do most national leaders, in fact, have some tremendous hangups which they take out on *us*? I really think so, at least in the case of RMN; but I would sure like to ask him this poem.

That's a lot of print to follow five lines, isn't it? The poem really does stand alone. You can't change a poem by talking about it, and you can't construct a poem because you have this nice formula. I had something to say, I wanted to say it well, and I said it, and I hope you like it.

Ron Ikan

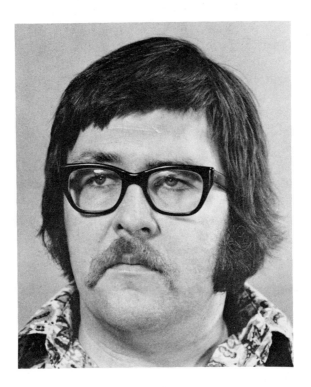

Born in 1941 in Waukegan, Illinois, Ron Ikan is presently living in Solon, Iowa. He has worked at various jobs: ditch digger, night cook, and section hand on the Rock Island Railroad. His poems have appeared in a number of publications including *Sport Magazine*.

BABYLON

The factories are pretending to be closed down for eternity.
The machines have accrued a lifetime of sick leave.
There are denim shirts dancing in roadhouse parking lots.
Australians and Chinamen are being recruited.

Environments are being melted down for the next war.
Sunshine cries out from its metal cage.
Metaphors are moving like cattle through hungry tunnels.
Are they thinking of setting poetry at a table?

Heaven and West Virginia are re-tooled.
Someone in the distance is screaming about rhinestones.
Books are buried in the graveyard of words.
Metro Goldwin Mayer is laughing, having breakfast.

SIDEWALK RESTORATION

The years of love in a parked car
were the highlights of his life. A string

of Cadillacs and wives with repossessed tears
slid him earthbound for the price

of bourbon, his secrets strewn like sawdust
in nickel dives; but in lamplight

the evil highway of his arm lay bare.
Filled with love and hate

that sudden night, Kansas City
flowing through his veins, he

was a little old for thirty-five,
a little young for death. Mingus came,

and Clayton Powell said some words
about the state of grace unsparingly

reserved in all-white plots.
As neon hopes and pawned belief

worked the eyeless length of street
someone thought they heard his horn

for one last time as free
and easy as a feather. Others

felt a grace note was received.
Waiting for grief in the Apollo balcony

they called upon the blues and thought
what an easy name Missouri was.

AMERICAN SATURDAY AFTERNOON

I am wondering how these first words will look
on the naked page. Even as I write them
a tenth of a million people cheer for Woody Hayes

and victory. A poet in Sioux City, Iowa has sent poems
in this morning's mail. Will he be burning the midnight oil tonight
of Moby Dick? This I will consider and consider and consider

as the crowd cheers and cheers and cheers. I will
go around with these few ideas until the crowd divines
water, or a school of whales, or a man

with candy and creased pants and a hang up
that would draw boos. I will stop then
and listen to the crowd, and perhaps even join them

in their beasthood. Then I will think of flint,
and of a million years ago. And if the poet in Sioux City
were here, we would smile and call it home.

ON "SIDEWALK RESTORATION"

I connect no philosophies to poetry in general or "Sidewalk Restoration" in particular. I trust "philosophy" as much as I trust used car salesmen and heads of state. I *do* trust what Whitman wrote and what Leadbelly sang and what Van Gogh painted.

The hero of "Sidewalk Restoration" is Charlie Parker. He played the saxophone the way no one else ever has and people used to call him Bird. I was fourteen when he died of an overdose of America. This poem was written fourteen years later. I wrote it because when I looked around I didn't see any statues of Bird and because of that solo on "Confirmation" where he makes the whole world stop. I think it's interesting how a true field nigger unloosens the writing hand.

Some of the things in the poem actually did happen: Mingus *was* at the funeral to bear the pall; Adam Clayton Powell *did* deliver the eulogy; Bird *was* thirty-five years old when he passed. I *don't* know if there was a stirring in the Apollo balcony that night or not, but I wouldn't want to bet against it. The blues has been rooted in North American blood for a long long time now, since, well, 1619 sounds about right.

Erica Jong

Born in 1942 in New York City, Erica Jong studied at Barnard and then at the Columbia School of the Arts with Mark Strand and Stanley Kunitz. Her first book, *Fruits & Vegetables*, was published by Holt, Rinehart, & Winston in 1971, the same year she won a grant from the New York State Council of the Arts and Cultural Council Foundation. She has taught workshops as well as literature and writing courses in this country and in Germany.

The Universal Explicator
hums softly to itself
the names of dreams
separates the hungers
sets them against each other

The Universal Explicator
grinds out bullets with its bowels
speeches with its mouths
air pollution
from every pore

The Universal Explicator
even makes love
with a choice of dildos
simultaneously makes war
simultaneously talks peace

The Universal Explicator
gives fellowships to bombs
& defense contracts to poets

A man once tried to murder it
His bullets boomeranged
& shot him dead
The Universal Explicator
canonized him instantly

The Universal Explicator
is tiny & fits
in the palm of your soul
If cornered will explode
inside you

THE MAN UNDER THE BED

The man under the bed
The man who has been there for years waiting
The man who waits for my floating bare foot
The man who is silent as dustballs riding the darkness
The man whose breath is the breathing of small white butterflies
The man whose breathing I hear when I pick up the phone
The man in the mirror whose breath blackens silver
The boneman in closets who rattles the mothballs
The man at the end of the end of the line

I met him tonight   I always meet him
He stands in the amber air of a bar
When the shrimp curl like beckoning fingers
& ride through the air on their toothpick skewers
When the ice cracks & I am about to fall through
he arranges his face around its hollows
he opens his pupilless eyes at me

For years he has waited to drag me down
& now he tells me
he has only waited to take me home
We waltz through the street like death & the maiden
We float through the wall of the wall of my room

If he's my dream he will fold back into my body
His breath writes letters of mist on the glass of my cheeks
I wrap myself around him like the darkness
I breathe into his mouth
& make him real

SIXTEEN WARNINGS IN SEARCH OF A FEMINIST POEM

1   Beware of the man who denounces ambition;
         his fingers itch under his gloves.

2   Beware of the man who denounces war
         through clenched teeth.

3   Beware of the man who denounces women writers;
  his penis is tiny & cannot spell.

4   Beware of the man who wants to protect you;
  he will protect you from everything but himself.

5   Beware of the man who loves your soul;
  he is a bullshitter.

6   Beware of the man who denounces his mother;
  he is a son of a bitch.

7   Beware of the man who spells son of a bitch as one word;
  he is a hack.

8   Beware of the man who loves death too well;
  he is taking out insurance.

9   Beware of the man who loves life too well;
  he is a fool.

10 Beware of the man who denounces psychiatrists;
  he is afraid.

11 Beware of the man who trusts psychiatrists;
  he is in hock.

12 Beware of the man who picks your dresses;
  he wants to wear them.

13 Beware of the man you think is harmless;
  he will surprise you.

14 Beware of the man who cares for nothing but books;
  he will run like a trickle of ink.

15 Beware of the man who writes flowery love letters;
  he is preparing for years of silence.

16 Beware of the man who praises liberated women;
  he is planning to quit his job.

134   *Erica Jong*

ON "THE MAN UNDER THE BED"

If I have a special fondness for this poem, it's partly because it was written quickly and partly because it took me my whole life to write.

As a child, I suffered from night terrors. I remember the panic about getting out of bed in the middle of the night for fear that some faceless phantom would drag me down to his lair under the bed. As an adolescent, I used to search all the closets before staying alone in the house at night. When I got married, I discovered that I could hardly sleep when my husband was away. But who was I afraid of? And why did I want him to come so badly? Despite years of talking to the ceiling of my analyst's office, it was this poem which finally domesticated my terror.

How did the poem get started?

I was reading *The Book of The It* by Georg Groddeck. In one of his imaginary letters, Groddeck's narrator, Patrik Troll, writes to his lady friend:

I said to you before: anxiety betokens a wish; whoever fears violation, desires it. Probably, if I know you aright, you also are not in the habit of searching under the beds and in the wardrobe; but how many women do this! Always with the fear and the wish to discover the man who is strong enough to have no terror of the law. You have heard before now the story of a lady, who, when she saw a man under her bed, broke out with the words, "At last! For twenty years I've been waiting for it!" How significant it is that this man is phantasied with a shining knife, a knife which is to be thrust into the body. . . ."

I was ready for Groddeck and Groddeck was ready for me. It was one of those rare moments of revelation. Of course, I thought, the man under the bed is a lover. The lover that every woman fears and desires. And desires because she fears. And then it all came in a flash. There was a different man under the bed for every stage of life. The bogey man for the little girl. The lover with the shining knife for the young woman. And death for the old woman. The last lover, the one whose embrace was fatal.

I thought of a very handsome man I knew whose perfect good looks had always terrified me. And suddenly I knew why: he corresponded with my unconscious image of the man under the bed.

With that, I began writing. It was late at night and very quiet and I wrote in a kind of trance, free-associating from one image to the next. I wrote without censoring, knowing I could cut out bad lines later. All I knew consciously was that I wanted a long rhythmic line, carried forward by an intense image, but the particular images (in the first stanza especially) were all summoned automatically and many of them later surprised me. (I discovered, for example, that I associated the man under the bed with *all* intruders, including obscene phone callers who merely— merely!—rape one's ear electronically). I knew that I wanted a somewhat dreamlike and incantatory feeling about the poem so I used the device of repetition rather than rhyme or any conventional meter. In the back of my mind were Christopher Smart's *Jubilate Agno* and Allen Ginsberg's *Howl*—two very different poems which nonetheless both use the device of repetition with great power. I muttered the poem to myself as I wrote; I heard the lines in my head.

When I'd finished the first draft, my notebook was a jumble of almost illegible words. I immediately began crossing out obviously weak and trite lines. Then I typed up the first somewhat revised draft. I thought it was either the worst or the best poem I'd ever written.

That Spring, I was in Stanley Kunitz' poetry seminar at The Columbia School of the Arts. We were due to meet a few nights later for the last class of the term—a sort of farewell party at the Kunitz' house. I brought along the man under the bed as my escort, but I swore to myself that he was too new to dare to read. I even brought along other poems in case I were called on. But, of course, when the time came, I reached for the man under the bed.

Carolyn Kizer was one of the guest poets present at that last meeting and she listened attentively as I read the poem through twice. Though the beginning of the poem was substantially as it is here, the ending was confused and badly overwritten. I read hesitantly, knowing that the ending was weak but not knowing how to fix it yet. It went:

His forehead is glass, clouds pass like goldfish
His boots hover slightly above the floor
His head pokes up through the smoke of the crowded room
The top of his head drifts off like last night's dream

For years he has waited to drag me down
& now he tells me
he has only waited to take me home
We waltz through the street like Death & the maiden
We float through the wall of the wall of my room

If he's my dream he will fold back into my body
My whole life I have been afraid of this
The reason I need him is easy: he's a bastard
He needs me to breathe in his mouth
& make him real

"The reason you need him is *not* easy," Carolyn Kizer said. "That's a beautiful poem ruined by a tacky Sylvia Plath ending." She was so clearly right, of course, that there wasn't much anyone wanted to add. The ending cheapened the poem, made it too schematic. But even more important, it was false. If the reason I needed him *were* easy, I'd never have written the poem.

Revisions (like the original process of writing itself) are not so much technical matters as they are matters of growth and self-discovery. When you suddenly discover that you can write a poem on a "subject" you couldn't handle before, it isn't because your "technique" has gotten better, but because your understanding of yourself has somehow grown. Perhaps "technique" for a poet is all a matter of self-discovery anyway. Clearly I had to go back to that secret (and scary) midnight place from which I write poems.

About ten days elapsed without my being able to summon another midnight interview with the man under the bed. I showed the poem to Patricia Goedicke, another poet-friend. "Too much explaining," she wrote next to the ending. And I knew she was right. The poem was meant to be evocative and dream-like, not explicit. I had ruined it by wanting to put everything in. I had made it a surrealist smorgasbord. I started cutting relentlessly.

Out went the silly glass forehead and the hovering boots. Out went the corny smoke-filled room. Out went the floating Salvadore Dali head. Out went the over-explicit phrase about "my whole life." Out went the tacky echo of Sylvia Plath's "Daddy" in the line, "The reason I need him is easy: he's a bastard." (It wasn't easy and maybe he wasn't even a bastard.) Finally, the crucial last two lines had to be dealt with. The man under the bed was a projection of *my* wish and I had to acknowledge that in order to revise the poem successfully. It was *I* who wanted to make love to the man under the bed. And all along I had been presenting myself as the innocent victim of a rape.

So the revision ultimately hinged on my own ability to be honest with myself—as indeed did the entire writing process. From fantasy to fear to rough draft to (hopefully) poem, every stage was linked to some sort of self-discovery, and to the ability to tolerate my knowledge of my own self-deceptions. Criticisms helped, of course, but only when I was ready for them. They wouldn't have helped at all otherwise.

After all this, how do I judge the poem? I don't know. And luckily it's not my job. I've done as much with it as I can for the moment, and other people seem to be moved by it. I've banished some of my own fears by giving them names and faces. Perhaps I've done the same for you.

R. P. Kingston

R. P.   Kingston was born in 1941 in Seattle, Washington. For the last
several years he has been in Boston working as a photographer and
writer of educational materials, and as an educational systems design
consultant. A Breadloaf Scholar in 1969, his poems have appeared in
Antioch Review, The Kansas Quarterly, South Dakota Review, and *The
Boston University Journal.*

Severed at the hip, Howard
hands himself along the floor,
his arms as thick as thighs
from doing double time,
his leftover body bound,
crab-like, at its waist
by a fat leather bucket
resting on one sole.

With a deft heave
and a shift of the spine,
he swings his stump of trunk
up from footprints he can't leave,
settles squarely into a booth,
and ordering coffee,
weighs the sleek waitress
on the edge of his eye:

Her legs
are ancient history.

MYSTIC LAKE

Once by a mountain lake high in the wilds
Of a Montana summer, searching the shallows
For sunken places that might hide a rainbow,
I followed a trail cut close to the shore

While my mind took another skirting deeper
Waters only just discovered. Out of place,
Out of time, the stillness was tangible,
Huge as the landscape. I rounded a curve:

There in the trail came a young woman walking,
Bare from the waist up, swinging her halter,
Appearing from nowhere. Surprise was our common ground,
Quick as a blow. In the space of an instant

We raced through a lifetime fused there together,
Each mirroring the other in glacial water.
Before I could speak, she was gone,
But the dream has stayed on.

BETWEEN TWO WARS

When warships anchored, spent in the Sound,
Searching for weather, waiting for new lives,
Mother ran a sheet out on the line.

In case it's your father's ship, she'd tell me;
And that lone sheet waited out the war with her,
Then settled at last, shaped to her still form.

Now Mother, back in Puget Sound
From a war of my own, waiting out the weather
With this grey fleet, I search the far shore

For signs of our lifetimes between two wars.
As the fog shifts to sea on a stiffening breeze,
I watch for a white sheet buried deep in years.

STATESIDE

In this most foreign of all places
Worn with faces hardened into stares,
The day careers down an endless street;
My feet set pebbles rattling from me;
Whole crowds pass through me; birds mock me;
Dust dogs my going to nights without rest:

Behind my eyes an aircraft carrier
Pushes into dawn upon an ocean
Balancing itself against the moon,
While, belly-full, its bombers climb
To grave heights, turning on their noses
In formation toward a scent of land.

140   R. P. Kingston

ON "HE'S KNOWN HIS LESSON FOR YEARS"

In "He's Known His Lesson For Years," which is one section of a long poem titled "Howard Elson Peace," I had a number of objectives, which changed a good deal as the poem developed toward completion.

Initially I simply wanted to write a poem about a man with no legs, and how he affected me and others around him, in a single setting. But over the several years during which the poem was written I began to get beneath the skin of my character, and new objectives and motivations presented themselves.

I began to see that what I was writing about was not a freak, not even a cripple, but an ordinary man forced by circumstances to live within extraordinary limitations, though in the eyes of others he was merely a something-less-than-human object of pity, curiosity, revulsion, and what have you; a neat package of generalizations. This central theme of the poem is stated later in the sequence: ". . . They won't believe/ a whole life will live in half of a body."

So the poem began to grow out of the vast difference between what I saw in the eyes of "They," those others around him, and what I came to see in his own eyes. The poem's tension comes out of the conflict between these opposing concepts of Self.

I first saw the man upon whom "Howard" is based in a coffee shop in Albuquerque, New Mexico, in 1967. Over a period of several months I saw this man perhaps a dozen times, always in the coffee shop (where I went evenings to write and drink infinitely refillable 10¢ cups of coffee). I never spoke to him; I never learned his name or any other personal fact about him (Howard Elson Peace is the name of an imaginary friend my younger brother created when he was a child); I simply watched.

In 1968 I moved to New England, and it was only with this distance that the poem got off the ground.

Technically, the poem is written in several forms, ranging from the free verse of "He's Known His Lesson For Years" to rhyming couplets, syntactic verse, amphrabraic dimeter, and a final sonnet.

In terms of voice and tone, I felt that Howard should speak for himself, that he was able to do so powerfully. Therefore, in "He's Known His Lesson For Years," as in each other section, I attempted merely to present a setting within which Howard could act, a setting as flat and two-dimensional as a picture, or a photograph. The sum of these pictures, or sections, would result, I felt, in a multi-dimensional figure greater than the sum of his parts, and—if I were lucky—one that came alive.

With the exception of the last two lines, "He's Known His Lesson For Years" is pure description. The only intrusion by the observer (the poet) is in his choice of descriptive elements, and the order in which he presents them. In the last two lines, "Her legs/ are ancient history," it is

Howard "speaking," or rather, the observer's impression of Howard's feeling as he "weighs the sleek waitress/ on the edge of his eye."

As far as the title is concerned, Howard's "Lesson" is all that I have been talking about: in the eyes of the world, he is an object, a freak, a "nigger" in the truest sense of the word. And the limitations imposed upon him are less a result of his physical disability than of the attitudes and blindness of people around him. And finally, as he illustrates in the last section of the poem, his lesson is that he can overcome not only these limitations, but also those constraints placed upon all human beings, and in realizing that, he reaches the millenium:

> ". . . I, Howard Elson Peace, am Einstein's child,
> I'm heir to his union with the universe. My
> bonds are all freed. The beast that howled
> at the heart of my being has lifted its curse,
> its sentence of life running out in my bones.
> [. . .]
> I'm accelerating to incredible size!"

Maxine Kumin

Maxine Kumin, novelist and poet, was born in Philadelphia, Pennsylvania in 1925. She has degrees from Radcliffe College and has been an instructor at Tufts University, a Scholar at the Radcliffe Institute for Independent Study, and a consultant to the Board of Coordinated Educational Services in Nassau County, New York. Her awards include the Lowell Mason Palmer Award from the Poetry Society of America and a grant from the National Council on the Arts and Humanities. Her novels are *The Passions of Uxport* (1968) and *Through Dooms of Love* (1965); her books of poems are *Halfway* (1961), *The Privilege* (1965), and *The Nightmare Factory* (1970). She presently lives in Newton Highlands, Massachusetts.

MORNING SWIM

Into my empty head there come
A cotton beach, a dock wherefrom

I set out, oily and nude
Through mist, in chilly solitude.

There was no line, no roof or floor
To tell the water from the air.

Night fog thick as terry cloth
Closed me in its fuzzy growth.

I hung my bathrobe on two pegs.
I took the lake between my legs.

Invaded and invader, I
Went overhand on that flat sky.

Fish twitched beneath me, quick and tame.
In their green zone they sang my name

And in the rhythm of the swim
I hummed a two-four-time slow hymn.

I hummed *Abide With Me*. The beat
Rose in the fine thrash of my feet,

Rose in the bubbles I put out
Slantwise, trailing through my mouth.

My bones drank water; water fell
Through all my doors. I was the well

That fed the lake that met my sea
In which I sang *Abide With Me*.

these are the dream machines
the dream machines
they put black ants in your bed
silverfish in your ears
they raise your father's corpse
they stick his bones in your sleep
or his stem or all thirty-six
of his stainless steel teeth
they line them up
like the best orchestra seats

these are the nightmare tools
down the assembly line
they send an ocean of feces
you swim in and wake from
with blood on your tongue
they build blind sockets
of subways and mine pits
for you to stop in
the walls slick as laundry soap
swelling and shrinking

these are the presses
they hum in nine languages
sing to the orphans
who eat pins for supper
the whole map of europe runs
hear the computers click
shunting the trains you take
onto dead sidings
under a sky that is
packed full of blackbirds

night after night
in the bowels of good citizens
nazis and cossacks ride
klansmen and judases
postmen with babies
heads down in their mailsacks

and for east asians
a new line of giants
dressed in g i fatigues
bayonets hooked in their ears

here on the drawing board
fingers and noses
leak from the air brush
maggots lie under
if i should die before
if i should die
in the back room
stacked up in smooth boxes
like soapflakes or tunafish
wait the undreamt of

THE PAWNBROKER

The symbol inside this poem is my father's feet
which, after fifty years of standing behind
the counter waiting on trade,
were tender and smooth and lay on the ironed sheet,
a study of white on white, like a dandy's shirt.
A little too precious; custom-made.
At the end of a day and all day Sunday they hurt.
Lying down, they were on his mind.

The sight of his children barefoot gave him a pain
—part anger, part wonder—as sharp as gravel
inside his lisle socks.
Polacks! he said, but meant it to mean
hod carriers, greenhorns, peasants; not ghetto Poles
once removed. *Where are your shoes? In hock?*
I grew up under the sign of those three gold balls
turning clockwise on their swivel.

Every good thing in my life was secondhand.
It smelled of having been owned before me by
a redcap porter whose ticket

ran out. I saw his time slip down like sand
in the glass that measured our breakfast eggs. At night
he overtook me in the thicket
and held me down and beat my black heart white
to make the pawnbroker's daughter pay.

On Saturday nights the lights stayed lit until ten.
There were cops outside on regular duty to let
the customers in and out.
I have said that my father's feet were graceful and clean.
They hurt when he turned the lock
on the cooks and chauffeurs and unlucky racetrack touts
and carwash attendants and laundresses and stock-
room boys and doormen in epaulets;

they hurt when he did up accounts in his head
at the bathroom sink
of the watches, cameras, typewriters, suitcases, guitars,
cheap diamond rings and thoroughbred
family silver, and matched them against the list
of hot goods from Headquarters,
meanwhile nailbrushing his knuckles and wrists
clean of the pawnticket stains of purple ink.

Firsthand I had from my father a love ingrown
tight as an oyster, and returned it
as secretly. From him firsthand
the grace of work, the sweat of it, the bone-
tired unfolding down from stress.
I was the bearer he paid up on demand
with one small pearl of selfhood. Portionless,
I am oystering still to earn it.

Not of the House of Rothschild, my father, my creditor
lay dead while they shaved his cheeks and blacked his
    mustache.
My lifetime appraiser, my first prince whom death un-
    horsed
lay soberly dressed and barefoot to be burned.
That night, my brothers and I forced

the cap on his bottle of twenty-year-old scotch
and drank ourselves on fire beforehand
for the sacrament of closing down the hatch,
for the sacrament of easing down the ways
my thumblicking peeler of cash on receipt of the
  merchandise,
possessor of miracles left unredeemed on the shelf
after thirty days,
giver and lender, no longer in hock to himself,
ruled off the balance sheet,
a man of great personal order
and small white feet.

ON "MORNING SWIM"

I dreamed the Muse came down one night, all bandaged and wearing a body cast, and reproached me for writing in form.

"All this plaster they've poured me into is your fault," she said. "You and your rhyme and meter have gotten me into this mess."

I protested. I quoted John Nims, who speaks of the poet's job as an act of "bending thought and rhythm until they touch."

But she only flailed at me with her crutch. "From now on it's free verse or nothing," she insisted.

It was in truth a learned nightmare.

Finally we compromised. She allowed me to choose one metrical pattern, and wild with reprieve I elected rhyming couplets.

Of this proscription "Morning Swim" came.

This is not quite a fable. Form in poetry gives me the freedom to grieve or rejoice. "Morning Swim" celebrates a sensuous moment. The restraint that the couplet form—here lightly, there sharply end-stopped—imposes makes it possible to hold the celebration.

Greg Kuzma

Greg Kuzma was born in Rome, New York in 1944. He received an M.A. from Syracuse University in 1967, and is now conducting poetry workshops at the University of Nebraska. He edits the magazine *Pebble* and *The Best Cellar Press* pamphlet series; he is also a contributing editor to *Prairie Schooner*. His poems have appeared in many publications.

HOSE AND IRON

It was always
father with the hose
and mother with the iron

then later it was
father with the iron
mother with the hose

but it was always
the hose and the iron

First, the hose:

Father said,
"when I was in
chemistry
this little guy came in
and all the wiseapples
were wisecracking
so he took out this hose
and bang on the desk
everybody shut up."

"The only way to treat kids."

Mother said,
"do you want your socks ironed
your pants ironed
your shirts
if you want those shirts ironed today
put them out for me
don't leave them balled up
on the stairway."

A long heavy hose
as big around as an arm
whack
they shut up

square shirts
pink yellow striped shirts
nice shirts

Hose me father
make me mind
hose me

iron me mother
I need to be ironed out

Father mother
I am dying of wisecracks

SLEEP

It has a name.
Your name, my name.
Some nights I walk around
in your sleep,
and you in mine.
We awake hopelessly tangled.

Some nights we cross
and do not recognize
each other.

Some nights we sleep
like two chairs
side by side.
A page keeps flopping
back and forth
across our seats.

I VISIT MY BROTHER

My brother stands among his friends
hoping I notice where his shoulders
are bare.
He wears a beautiful mask of surrender.
He has surrendered
to everything weak in the world
calling it good
and everything kind in the world
calling it love.
His mind has given his body
a new landscape
in which to lose itself.
He wears the small garments
of peace.
Birds sing louder here.
The grass engulfs them.
I pace back and forth
like a failure.
But no one is astonished.

AH

What not one poem yet
here having left you
hours ago with plenty
of paper
up to your fish damp face
in paper and hungry.
Not one poor poem
to rush off sealed
away in paper
to be read in an office
stacked with paper by
paper faces
to result in things
like I like this paper

Kuzma he makes some nice
paper did you see his
paper in the XXX
Paper Journal
quite papery.
Or I have never been
turned on by your paper
but this new paper on
your elaborately casual
paper I think splendid.
I will try to fit it
into my next paper.

Oh Kuzma your name
does not move you
there is not enough paper
stacked in the other room
you have not touched
your pen to sufficient
paper to bring out
all the paper within
you
you will never come down
to yourself because of
precisely this paper.
You will live in misery
wrestling with yourself
on paper
and between papers or
on your way to the paper
or on your way back
from the paper.

Confess it
you hate your life.

FIRST CAMP

Late at night
the fire has come down
from its inches of flame
to lie along the ground.

Above me the tent is breathing;
the sky moves out and in.
I hear a thousand porcupines
gnawing at the darkness.
Far off in the woods
an owl no longer hungry
shakes it out of his feathers.

Something swims on the lake.
Now it is skimming the surface,
now it is limp as a lily pad.
I roll in my covers
like an animal warm to his den.

Something skits across
the edge of camp.
I think: rabbit or mouse.
Then it is morning.
I duck my head in the blue water.
Then it is night.
Then it is morning again.

ON "I VISIT MY BROTHER"

"I Visit My Brother" is, of course, a poem which depends almost completely on something quite private. It recounts a single meeting between us, but tries also to give a feel of the relationship in general. Let me say something about what's behind or "inside" the poem. My brother is eight years younger than I, and had the difficulty of having to grow up following me as well as into a more difficult age. In high school in the late fifties all that mattered to my friends and me and our parents was getting through with good grades and on to college and a job. Around the time I was halfway through college and becoming, like many other people, dissatisfied and slightly rebellious, I began wearing a beard, writing poems, and not keeping things up so much as I had. So Jeff had what my parents saw as my gradually disintegrating example as well as those of his peers, a lot of "lazy" kids who might have been branded punks eight years earlier, but who were not so easy to reckon with through the new kinds of rhetoric and concern. When he turned from the sort of future I had at first envisioned for myself he turned hard—in a sense carrying through on the rebellion I was merely dallying with.

What I try to show in the poem are some of the things about us that are important. One, that he had founded for himself, by the time of the visit, a life as secure as anything I believed I had. And that, among his friends, where I find him in the poem, he is proud of his freedom, his self, perhaps for the first time in front of me. While I want to show this I also recognize how much of what I see is a style, a cliché, how much he has assumed to cover him, not grown into or earned. I am critical of him, of his belief that he is more real, more in touch with things, more at peace than I am. The poem intends not to finalize a single position but rather to display the width of the conflict. The nagging description of him in his world is meant to balance with the judgment levelled against me at the end of the poem. My nervousness in the situation is seen by the others as the natural result of my values—an all too typical reaction given the style I attribute to them. The word "astonished" tries to cut a couple ways—it is too strong a word in the context, but it is one which I supply, a product of my discomfort, and it tries to work to picture them sitting complacently, unaware of what I sense in the scene. The others have an immunity to the meeting, and their lack of astonishment is meant to suggest, I hope, how what matters is unresolved. And I too am included in the "no one."

Were I to develop the poem further I might try to carry it along two lines, the failures of my own life, one of which was my inability to look after my brother in any helpful way, and that of the complacency of his understanding. I leave it where it is because it rubs right like this, and because it is still too early to write about how things have come out. Written three years ago it still accounts for much of what exists between us.

If some of this is working for the reader of the poem then perhaps it is because the sentences, following line by line in sequence, but also in parallel, serve as uncommitted givens. Nothing is stressed over anything else—I try merely to present things one on top of another, to try to recapture the simultaneity of my ambiguous reactions. Most of my poems develop not out of plans for poems but rather out of a world of words and things that are not in words but straining to be. Whatever I offer here is more the result of having the poem to look through after having written it and having felt satisfied that some of these things had been given shape and voice.

Larry Levis

Larry Levis was born in 1946 in Fresno, California where he grew up on a farm. Taking courses under the poet Philip Levine at Fresno State College made him decide to write poetry. He also attended Syracuse University and studied with the poets Philip Booth and Donald Justice. He has been a mill worker, a dishwasher, and a farm hand, but prefers teaching. Currently he is teaching at California State College in Los Angeles. His first book, *Wrecking Crew* (1972), won the 1971 United States Award for Poetry. His work has appeared in periodicals such as *Northwest Review, Hearse, Intro 2, Choice,* and *TransPacific.*

THE POEM YOU ASKED FOR

My poem would eat nothing.
I tried giving it water
but it said no,

worrying me.
Day after day,
I held it up to the light,

turning it over,
but it only pressed its lips
more tightly together.

It grew sullen, like a toad
through with being teased.
I offered it all my money,

my clothes, my car with a full tank.
But the poem stared at the floor.
Finally I cupped it in

my hands, and carried it gently
out into the soft air, into the
evening traffic, wondering how

to end things between us.
For now it had begun breathing,
putting on more and

more hard rings of flesh.
And the poem demanded the food,
it drank up all the water,

beat me and took my money,
tore the faded clothes
off my back,

said Shit,
and walked slowly away,
slicking its hair down.

Said it was going
over to your place.

FOR THE COUNTRY

I

One of them undid your blouse, then
used a pocket knife to
cut away your skirt
like he'd take
fur off some limp thing,
or slice up the belly of a fish.

Pools of rainwater shone in the sunlight,
and they took turns.

II

After it was over,
you stared up, maybe,
at the blue sky where the shingles were missing,
the only sounds
pigeons
walking the rafters, their eyes fixed, shining,
the sound of water dripping.
The idiot drool of the cattle. Flies.

III

You are the sweet, pregnant,
teen-age blonde thrown from the speeding car.

You are a dead, clean-shaven astronaut
orbiting perfectly forever.

You are America.
You are nobody.
I made you up.
I take pills and drive a flammable truck
until I drop.

I am the nicest guy in the world,
closing his switchblade and whistling.

IV

The plum blossoms have
been driven into a silence all
their own,
as I go on
driving an old red tractor
with a busted seat.
The teeth of its gears
chatter in the faint language
of mad farm wives who have whittled,
and sung tunelessly,
over the dog turds in their front yards,
for the last hundred years.

V

And I will say nothing, anymore, of
my country,
nor of my wife reading about abortions,
nor of the birds that
have circled high over my
head, following me,
for days.

I will close my eyes,
and grit my teeth,
and slump down further in
my chair,
and watch what goes on
behind my eyelids:
stare at the dead horses with flowers stuck in
their mouths—

and that is the end of it.

I will stuff a small rag of
its sky into my pocket forever.

ON "THE POEM YOU ASKED FOR"

Nobody asked for "The Poem You Asked For." I certainly didn't. All
day I'd been trying to write a "big" poem, something of terrific im-
portance which would in some vague way affirm and validate my life.
Anyway, nothing happened. The desk I shared with three other teachers
at Fresno State College became blanker and blanker. I had been going
through a period of not writing and was disgusted with myself. As a poet
I can let anything from two weeks to a summer drift by and feel almost
peaceful about it. Then I'll get tough with myself and go back to work.
And sometimes nothing will come. At the worst this makes me surly
and depressed enough to forget the whole thing and wait for rain. But
sometimes, too, in the moments of a stale inward rage which is like beads
of water evaporating in a jar, a kind of grace can occur. I find I have no
ideas, I find myself watching things, nothing very important. With luck,
I can become unimportant enough to write a poem.

I finally gave up on the big poem that day, and got on a bus to go
home. The children playing in the back seat ignored the driver's grunts
and demands for silence. The door, with its sound of sighing, opened
and closed. The taut barracks of the suburbs drifted by in the heat. And
this poem began its arrogant dance, and I was open or defeated enough
to hear it.

It is not an important poem, I think. But it is a poem, and the process
of writing it, or of writing any poem I feel good about, puts me in touch
with my own sweet life. At home I showed the poem to my wife, and we
laughed and sat down to dinner.

Thomas Lux

Thomas Lux was born in 1946 in Massachusetts. He graduated from Emerson College in Boston in 1970, and is currently living in Iowa City, Iowa where he is managing editor of *The Iowa Review* and an editor for Barn Dream Press. His poems have recently appeared in *Kayak, New American Review, Field, Hearse, Massachusetts Review, The Beloit Poetry Journal,* and *Lillabulero.* Pym-Randall Press has published both a pamphlet and a full-length collection of his poems entitled *Memory's Hand Grenade* (1972).

IF YOU SEE THIS MAN

Notify someone of authority
if you see this man:

He has a fish hook
in his upper lip.
He usually carries a bleeding starfish
in a dixie cup.
He is an excellent fork-lift
operator and is known
to play dice with nuns.
He is big.
He claims to detest golf coaches.

We want him for the robbery
of the first kiss ever given
to a bus driver's sickly daughter.

And remember, he is ruthless.
If he knew you had read this
he would murder you.

GOING HOME

Sitting at the kitchen table
I look out the front door
and across the road
and see five cows.
These are just the cows I can see
through the front door.
Now you can imagine how big the herd is.

One old cow, a guernsey, walks
to the edge of the road
and sticks her head through the fence.
She begins dragging her huge black lip
across the asphalt.

She opens her mouth and cars drive in!
Lost motorists wade
across her tongue, I hear tire irons
bang against her teeth,
her teeth as flat as coins . . .

My father is sitting across from me.
He won't look. He says
he has seen entire herds yawning like this,
swallowing houses, families,
the enormous combines. . . .

He says to me O the dark throat!,
the giant yellow eyes, on fire!

We dance all night in the kitchen.
We drink to this country, we spit in her face.

SOME ORAL STANZAS

Her shoulder is in your mouth.

A very thin lozenge of butter
is about to fly
into your mouth.

In your mouth
the heart of a chicken is dissolving.

In your mouth
there is a factory of cave paintings.

You believe
an empty, refrigerated boxcar
is parked in your mouth.

A blind animal
perhaps a lavish insect,
begs to live in your mouth.

Her shoulder is in your mouth.

HOW TO CURE YOUR FEVER

Pull your bed aside and dig
a hole in the dirt floor.

Trick your wife, the one you divorced
a hundred years ago, so that
she falls asleep in this hole.

Replace as much dirt as possible.

Now drag the bed back
and center it over the spot.

As your fever subsides
think of the lawnmower in your heart,
try not to freeze—

FIVE MEN I KNOW

One has fallen drunk
across the instrument panel of my life.
I can't read the dials.
I don't know how much energy I have—

Another one dreams
he is reading the *Duino Elegies* aloud,
in German, at a racetrack in Florida.
In his dream
the flamingoes are drained of their color
and collapse.

A third one lives in a gaunt library,
more like a blue tunnel, sinking.
He also dreams: O to be a lieutenant!
When he is not reading
he is asleep,
dreaming: to be a lieutenant!, O a leader
of insipid platoons!

The next one woke up
and half his house was gone.
Half his desk, his chair, his table,
half of everything was gone.
A small pile of snow
was crowding him, on what was left of the bed.

The last one is being chased by a man
with a hammer. The man running
wears a body-cast.
He has been wearing it for centuries.
The man with the hammer
wants to remove it.

ON "FIVE MEN I KNOW"

The title of the poem helps make its intent a little clearer. It's a five
stanza poem about five different men, or, five different poems. I hope
that it works both ways. I hope the tone, if it's to be taken as five differ-
ent poems, runs a thread through it. Each stanza describes a different
man. There are two men in the first stanza. One of them is a narrator
and is involved only slightly. The man described obviously interferes
with the narrator's life. He drinks too much. He falls down. The second
man is probably the hardest to explain. I can only *show* you what he is,
what he does. Obviously, he is a fan of Rilke's. He is a horse racing fan.
He is, for some reason, bitter. The man in the third stanza is twisted.
Living in a gaunt place, a blue tunnel, has twisted him. He'd rather
be a fish, no, a bird, no . . . The next man is easier to explain. His stanza
is concerned with loss. He has somehow lost half his life. Two men are
again involved in the last stanza. One of them, the man with the ham-
mer, is as unimportant as the narrator in the first stanza. The important
man in this stanza is encased in a body-cast. He can still run. His body-
cast, and many other images in this poem are metaphorical or associative.
I hope that the reader finds them close to *his* life, but I can only describe
these men, and then, only briefly. I can show you what I know about
them, a glimpse into their lives. If I could explain them fully I'd be a
psychiatrist, or a prince. I can only try to make them as clear as possible.

Morton Marcus

Morton Marcus was born in New York City in 1936 and has a B.A. from the University of Iowa. He served in the U.S. Air Force from 1954 to 1958. His work has been published in many magazines as well as in over twenty anthologies. He is the author of three collections of poems: *Origins* (1969), *Where the Oceans Cover Us* (1972), and *The Santa Cruz Mountain Poems* (1972).

PROVERBS

who drowns an ocean
wakes in a desert

who cuts a tree's throat
is imprisoned in air

who murders a mountain
is condemned to the ground

who impersonates one
is really two

who is really one
is more than a number

who speaks to the silence
creates a mountain

who listens to trees
hears the speech of his father

who prays to an ocean
is reborn in the waters

FAMILY GAME

a shadow
flutters
through
the forest

I will hunt
it down
says
the man

I will kiss
its mouth
says
his wife

we will find
its breath
say
the children

already
their heads
are drifting
apart

darkened
lanterns
in the
forest

2 POEMS WRITTEN ON TURNING AROUND
TOO QUICKLY WHILE HIKING

with apologies to James Wright

I

Whenever I move
my body leaves a cave behind me.
Perhaps someone
(a lost dog, a bobcat,
maybe lovers)
will find refuge in it
for a moment,
or even
a night's sleep.

II

With each step
I leave behind someone familiar—
an old coat hung out in the wind,
shoulders sagging.
"Why have you stopped, old man,
we've a long way to travel."
He stands there, not replying.
Behind him there are others,
all dressed alike,
for as far as I can remember.

HAND

Thumb

blind bald-headed blunderer
moron I might have become
eyes nose mouth stopped up
with cushions of flesh
an impermeable thickness
ideas cannot enter
         blunt as the infant
         squatting at the village edge
         oblivious to passersby

Index

the pointer
full of possibilities
lean and muscular
with impatient energies
traces the words in books
and soon will be going
         explorer visionary
         builder of roads and bridges
         now lifter of latches opener of doors

Middle

bachelor with bizarre habits
owns the largest house
in the village
has never traveled
yet speaks of mysterious dungeons
that only he is able to reach

         and yet his explorations
         have not made him
         cynical or cruel

Ring

married burdened with bills
awkward and short of breath
sits in a large chair
staring out the window
while his children laugh
and run through the house

         or reads his brother's letters
         which tell of cities
         set like jewels beyond the mountains

Little

inquisitive old man
clean and well-mannered
bent like a question
he never asks aloud
lives alone at the end
of the village thinking

         "these are my people
         in this valley I kissed the wind
         and caged the sun in my hands"

ON "HAND" AND "PROVERBS"

It is difficult for me to speak about the craftsmanship involved in any one of these poems, since craft is a mysterious, shaping force to me—an intuitive molding that goes on while the poem is being written.

Olson has it right, I think, when he says that structure is an extension of content. Closed-form poetry, on the other hand, is a known territory, and that territory is the limitation of the form in which the poet is working. But when structure becomes an extension of content all boundaries are destroyed, and the poet, like an explorer, is plunged into the country inside himself, which is beyond the frontiers of the known. This is the excitement of open-form poetry being written in America today: the constant *self* (and therefore *cultural*) discoveries the poet makes through meanings being expressed as new forms, the infinite possibilities existing in the universe inside him.

This is not as radical as it may sound. No experimentation is. The tools of poetry, as opposed to the forms, remain generally the same—the resources of one's language, figurative speech, and a known syntax. True one can, and maybe should, create new word combinations and new syntactical structures, but these must always rely on the known (a new tool is made by modifying an old one). The whole question of open forms can be seen in terms of the "tool" metaphor, for in this argument our tools are what we work with, but the designs we make with them can be from either preconceived patterns (closed forms) or from new ones created by guiding the tools with vision, intuition, or automatic (i.e., "unconscious") action.

All this implies a hit-or-miss, intuitive technique on the part of the poet. He must constantly try out new directions of feeling, thought, association, expression, and usage. Much of the time the result will be a failure, but the exhilaration of finding new trails, even if they are dead ends, will sustain him. The world remains open. Everything is possible. The attempt is all.

It follows that I did not know how any of these poems was going to turn out, neither structurally nor thematically. In fact, I didn't even know what I was writing about until I was more than halfway through the first draft, which is usual procedure with me. The writing takes over. I start with a rhythm, a word, usually an image. "Hand" wrote itself for the first two stanzas. Oddly enough, this poem is written in what must be considered a closed form, as I set up a stanza with a specific number of lines in a seemingly arbitrary fashion, which something inside me said must be adhered to. But this was not planned beforehand: the first two stanzas just came out that way, both in nine lines, the last three in each case being a new direction in tone and syntax. The pattern was set. But when I realized what I was about, and tried to work out both form and metaphor for the middle finger, the pivotal stanza of the poem, I could sense the strain. That stanza is the worst in the poem, as far as I'm concerned. Luckily, the poem picked up again in the last two stanzas. Generally I knew that each line would be a unit of breath, which usually winds up being a phrase in my poetry. This self-imposed rule gets fuzzy not only in the middle stanza, but in the last as well, in which lines five and six should read

> lives alone at the end of the village
> thinking

but by this time "the form" was set, and a world of infinite possibilities became a walled village.

I was aware of the village image and the emblematic symbols usually assigned to the index, middle and ring fingers as I wrote, but "the five ages of man" theme eluded my conscious mind until I came to the ring finger and wrote the word "married." I didn't know what the little finger was going to do, but when he began to speak as a lonely old patriarch celebrating his existence I was delighted. And when he delivered the last line, in which the whole poem suddenly turns back on its own metaphor, I was (and this is one of the joys of poetry to me) pleasantly shocked. Originally the word "valley" in the last stanza was "village," but the poet Robin Magowan pointed out that the idea of a valley beyond the village would cause the poem to expand in the reader's imagination instead of stop there. The least important aspect of the poem is its physical design, but since it exists it deserves some comment. The last three lines of each stanza were new sentences in different rhythms from the first six, and when I indented them, which I did for no apparent reason as I wrote the original draft, they seemed to make a stylized picture of a hand.

In a similar fashion, "Proverbs" is also a closed form. It is in couplets. The lines are more equal rhythmically than the lines in "Hand" but the form is much simpler, with the first line of each stanza containing the subject of the sentence and the second the predicate. The poem began as a series of images, each a separate proverb, but when I wrote the fifth stanza I realized the proverbs were shaping themselves into a structure, a poem, and that the poem was turning back on itself to re-examine from a positive point of view the images which had been negatively stated in the first four.

William Matthews

William Matthews was born in Cincinatti, Ohio in 1942. He has a B.A. from Yale and an M.A. from the University of North Carolina at Chapel Hill, and has been teaching writing courses at Cornell University since 1969. He is co-founder and co-editor of Lillabulero Press and its magazine *Lillabulero*. His published books are *Broken Syllables* (1969), *Ruining the New Road* (1970), *The Cloud* (1971), and *The Waste Carpet* (1971).

YOUR EYES, YOUR NAME

I

These words we have swallowed—
blind fish in an underground lake.
One dies up into your eyes
like a stone bubble.
Love offers miraculous
exactions. I lean to this dank
flame of no fire,
I try to name it.

II

More light, I cried, as Goethe
did from his deathbed.
It sounded beautiful and true.
But it's one thing to go blind
if you're about to die.
And here I am, two frank
explosions in your eyes.
This close you become—in its
fervency—the light I give you back.
Now I know what to say:
your name, true title
to this poem. I'll love you
as well as you'll let me.
More light. More darkness, too.

III

So it must be late
afternoon, kiss me.
Your small mouth is beautiful.
Your eyes close.
Tongues, eels
of shy light—they are names
learning to pronounce each other.

IV

Now it's night. Our light
is prickling through it
like fire along the veins
of a deserted coalmine.
A storm would be appropriate.
After a storm the earth
and I are delirious with ease.
I close my eyes.

Lightning chars the air sweet
and original, and so does sleep.

V

I'd like to name a book of poems
Foreplay. One poem unbuttons
your interpretation of it.
Another's breath smells of a toothpaste blended
from raspberries and Romanée-Conti, 1959,
and this poem is the best kisser.
Another is a hand of light
staining a dark breast.
One is a willful tongue
and will creep anywhere along your body.
Each poem has a beautiful hobby.
They are like blankets we have kicked away,
a mound
knit from the last notes
sung before the silence
these poems have always loved.

BLUES FOR JOHN COLTRANE, DEAD AT 41

Although my house floats on a lawn
as plush as a starlet's body
and my sons sleep easily,

I think of death's salmon breath
leaping back up the saxophone
with its wet kiss.

Hearing him dead,
I feel it in my feet
as if the house were rocked
by waves from a soundless speedboat
planing by, full throttle.

PRAISE

First, to the feet, as they bear what you have grown
    to live in, your pod of a body, slow to explode.

And to the toes, as they were roots once, and so you
    go by me like a bush of bells searching for music,
    and I sing in my bad voice *hello* and we turn to
    each other.

And to the calves, as their long canoe-shaped muscles
    glide in the same place always over the sunken bone,
    the body's future.

And to the knees, as they are loud echoes of the knuckles
    and the backs of them grow pink and painful if you fall
    asleep face-down in the sun.

When the thighs are drunk on duty and I creep by, I tell
    them a strange dream and they have it and are re-
    freshed. Praise to the thighs, stolid and lovely.

And to the buttocks, as they bob like pans of a scale
    when you walk away and take my true weight when I
    lie down on you.

And to the hips, as every cup should have a handle, as they
    are the ears and ankles of the body's delta, as they
    are your calcium outriggers covered by flesh.

And to the navel, as it is the first crater. Its seal is
    all that's left of your mother's letter explaining
    happiness and pain. Praise to the navel.

And to the *linea alba,* as it is bellrope for the pubic hair
    and the tongue's path to music lessons.

And to the clitoris, as it is a loaf of tiny bread, a pearl
    of blood, because it does nothing but drum and trouble
    the inner waters.

And to the cunt, as it is the glove that is mother to the
    finger, mouth that gives speech to the tongue, home
    that gives restlessness to the cock.

And to the stomach, as it contains the speech your body
    makes to itself, boring as can be, every day of hun-
    ger: *Fill me, I am empty with the knowledge of my
    need.*

And to the back, as the dunes of muscles shift across it,
    and that underground river of bones, your spine, flows
    through it.

And to the shoulders, as they were wings once. Your shoulders
    gather like dense clouds that are moored by rain to the
    rest of your body, and I praise the way they float there.

And to the breasts, as they doze waiting for babies, as
    the nipples sting in cold wind, as a hand or tongue,
    like a shadow with the right weight, passes over
    them.

And to the throat, as it is the stalk of your face and the
    place where your breath breaks into the right syllables:
    I place my tongue on your throat's bluest vein, in
    praise.

And to the tongue, as it lolls and darts on its tether—
    domestic, secret, blunt.

And to the lips, as my name or anything you say blooms
    on them to die away. When I kiss you I leave my name
    again for your breath to pass through.

And to the nose, as it remembers and uses fumes from the
    fire of the arriving future.

And to the ears, as their delicate bones shiver precisely;
    they are shells listening to themselves, and they can
    hear the roar of the blood always.

When I stare into your eyes, a little knot of light in mine
    breaks. Undressing the light, we see that darkness is
    its birthmark. Praise to the eyes.

And to the hair, as when I sift it with my fingers it re-
    members its first life as grass on the early earth
    and springs back to its own shape.

And to the arms, as they hold in order to let go. We rock
    in the boats of our bodies. The wind rises, the final
    lust. When you raise your arms, the space between them
    is a sail I helped to sew.

And to the hands, as their cargo of scars and air can never
    be given away. You may rest them on my body if you
    like.

And to the fingers, as they are failed tunnels into nothing-
    ness. They went a little way and came home to the body.

And to the bones, the body's ore and its memory of itself
    when the rest of it is the breath of something else—
    to the bones, praise.

And to the face, as light flares and calms between the skin and
    skull. And those blind cows, my fingers, graze there in any
    weather.

And to the blood, tireless needle pulling its thread of
    tides, tireless praise. Say it again and again,
    the names are lying down to sleep together.

ON "PRAISE"

Usually I begin a poem with a few words or an image. Then, since I don't know if I'm at the beginning or end or somewhere else in the eventual poem, I write outward, as if in circles, until the poem begins, blurrily, to make its own shape. Then I try to be as faithful to that as I can. Often the first thing I wrote down has been crossed off.

As a result, my poems remain formally surprising to me as they are being written. I like to find in them things and situations I don't already know. But, writing "Praise," when I wrote the first word, "First," I knew I wanted to use a recurring form. I had been writing some love poems in which the costs and losses and deceptions of love had kept asserting themselves, and I wanted to write a poem of praise. So the litany form seemed right.

In most poems—certainly in most of mine—the line moves out from the margin, as if testing all that silence, then ducks back to start again. So that while the line's first motion is outward, its deeper motion is, however sidelong and serpentine, downward. But there is another line— Whitman's is an example—which is like a fishing line. You throw it out as far as it will go. This line assumes there will be a place to land; i.e., it assumes the amplitude of the universe. Since I wanted in my poem not only to praise the various parts of a woman's body, but also to celebrate that amplitude, I found myself using this longer, more outward line. Maybe I even chose to begin at the feet and go upward as a way of de- claring independence from the usual downward line. I know I chose to begin with the feet to reverse the procedure of the textbook high school seduction, since I didn't want the poem to have that—or only that—rela- tionship to the body.

Twice, at the thighs and again at the eyes, the poem breaks its habit of beginning each new line with "And." I make such decisions intuitively when I'm writing a poem, but, looking back, I often see good reason for them. Linguists call the mode of linking syntax with "and" *parataxis,* from the Greek for "placing side by side." It doesn't indicate hierarchical relationships between clauses by words like *but, however,* or *next,* nor by parallel or antithetical construction. The time in such syntax is a kind of expanded, or suspended, present. And yet the body exists in fluid time, and the poem's imagery keeps insisting that the body dies in fluid time. The body "explodes"; the bones are the body's "memory of itself when the rest of it is the breath of something else." So I began those two lines with "When." Intense awareness of the body expands our sense of the present (that which is given), but that awareness should in- clude the knowledge of death.

Imagining a woman's body, a man is writing about something *other.* Recognizing this element of confrontation, I put myself into the poem.

But the poem isn't personal in the way that a love poem is, or a poem about my reaction to the death of a jazz musician. Its imagery doesn't point to the uniqueness of the individual: the woman could be any woman, or perhaps a composite of real and imagined women. There are nautical images—canoe, outrigger, sailboat—perhaps because the body is the ship of death. There are musical images—bells, music lessons, a drum, the bones of the ear—related to images of speech and silence. There are images in which the body imitates itself—the knees "echo" the knuckles, and hips are like ears and ankles. Mostly the images link the body to landscape. The body is a pod, the navel a crater, the bones in one place an underground river and in another ore. The throat is a stalk, the tongue a tethered animal. Hair is grass and blood is the sea. Underneath this poem is a metaphor which is never stated directly: the body and the planet are somehow the same thing. Surely we inherit at birth loyalties to the body and to the planet which supersede and outlast all other loyalties. These others—to governments, to institutions, to family—are learned, and we are most likely to resist them when they ask us to turn from our bodies and the planet.

Most of the formal decisions I made writing the poem, I now think, grew from the influence of the poem's unstated central metaphor. They also grew from the desire to praise. Somehow it seems easier to write out of grief and loss than out of joy. The world is always telling us to be cheerful, not to take things personally, to be reasonable. Many poets and thinkers have spoken of an inner self, one who resists spurious reassurance and attacks false spirituality. I think most good lyric poems are written by this self. For this reason many theories of art locate the imagination in the inner self. But I think the imagination is everywhere, and that its life-work is to accommodate to each other the inner and outer selves. Jung called the inner self a "shadow self" and proposed that it was the opposite sex to the outer self. Maybe that's why my poem *is*, after all, a seduction poem. It's a prayer for the peace that comes when the names lie down to sleep together, and, because names are magical, the parts of the body and the inner and outer selves lie down, too, side by side. Good night.

Tom McKeown

Tom McKeown was born in 1937. Educated at the University of Michigan, he has taught at Alpena College in Michigan and Wisconsin State University. Currently he is teaching creative writing at Stephens College in Columbia, Missouri. He has traveled extensively outside the United States. His poems have appeared in publications such as *The New Yorker, The Nation, Commonweal, New York Quarterly, Kayak, Southern Poetry Review,* as well as in several pamphlets.

THE BUFFALO, OUR SACRED BEAST

I dream millions of buffalo
moving across the plains.
Everywhere they crush the cities
that have taken their land,
everywhere they announce
our end is near, everywhere
they herd us into the sea.
I am running with them
through the streets, drunk
on buffalo milk and nourished
by dung.
I carry a flag with a buffalo on it
and on my staff I spin a human skull.
There is no way to save you,
though I have tried,
no chance to save you from this truth.

WOMAN WITH FINGER

If you
have seen her,
then you know
that birds fly out
of her mouth

and light sleeps
in her hair.

Her finger
keeps making
circles
within circles,

movements
I cannot follow.

I imagine I see
her finger
tracing the night sky.

She has told me
that the night sky
is her invention

and her finger
a line in my poem.

1937 FORD CONVERTIBLE

Rusted and without tires
it rests on the side of a hill,
abandoned like an ugly bride,
tangled in thorns and high weeds.
It has lost its glass
and even the desire for roads.
I sit in the cracked front seat
and contemplate my life: stalled,
overturned, pointing
toward the factory
far down the hill.

ON "WOMAN WITH FINGER"

This poem was written a number of years ago before I had read Lorca.
The phantasmagorical woman with the creative finger. Perhaps the en-
tire poem is about one thing: imagination. Perhaps not.

It starts out: "If you have seen her," that is, if you have experienced
this other world, then you may see/feel the other unworldly things. The
woman (imagination) moves at a fantastic speed, a speed which we can-
not follow or comprehend. Then the "I" (the poet) imagines what she
(the imagination) is doing. The circles within circles is the labyrinth
that this other world throws in front of us. A labyrinth in which we are
lost. A beautiful, lost world.

There is a sense of movement in the poem, movement unrestrained. The woman goes on and on until she is beyond us, until her finger is even a line in the poem itself. The imagination is making itself known. Things happen without reason, cause or anything. Things simply happen, conditions arrive. And we wait. With Keats (perhaps) under a tree. Attempting to empty our minds, attempting to open ourselves to whatever is there, beyond ourselves. Perhaps there is something to *negative capability*? Something else is out there, I can feel it.

The woman of the poem is beautiful because of her wild power, her grace, her motion, her knowledge. She is even the creator of the night sky. Darkness is her beauty as well as light. The "I" of the poem is passive. If she has made the circles, let birds fly out of her mouth, has light in her hair, invented the night sky, and if one of her fingers is a line in the poem, then perhaps the entire poem is her invention too. And thus the "I" (poet) is merely a vehicle by which that other world is revealed.

This poem made itself in my sleep (let Coleridge sleep, please) and I wrote the poem down quickly before I was fully awake. It took several days before I got the last two lines. I didn't intend these lines to be tricky. I feel the poem works up to the ending. Birds coming out of her mouth at the beginning, awakens us to a myriad of possibilities which are partly fulfilled in the body of the poem, but not fully realized until the last two lines.

I like poetry that embodies the supernatural and the occult. Usually the poem of the unconscious is the poem that does something. It is not a poem which is built by craft, as such. There is always another dimension. Although one must have some sense of and facility with language, one must be receptive to the inner world of images and feelings and be ready to gather them as they drift up occasionally from the depths. "Woman With Finger" floated up out of the depths already made and was written down, just as it was beginning to dissolve into a quiet summer morning freckled with light.

William Pitt Root

William Pitt Root writes:

    Born in a blizzard shortly after Christmas, 1941, Austin, Minnesota, but raised around my father's farms on the edge of the Everglades up to 1955, then to Seattle. Since high school, I've lived and worked up and down the west coast, North Carolina, Pennsylvania, Michigan, Vermont, travelled in Europe, making my living at factory work, teaching, poetry readings, as a teamster, maitre d', bouncer, married for four years and divorced, lived a while communally, hit 30 on a sunny day in the dead of winter.

Mr. Root has a B.A. from the University of Washington and an M.F.A. from the University of North Carolina. He was a Wallace Stegner Fellow in 1971. He is the author of *The Storm and Other Poems* (1967).

THE HOUSE YOU LOOKED FOR

I

Upstate New York.
  That haunts me still—beginning
our late fall walk in fields of blown gold weeds
and trees blown red and gold.

That time, that trip to your old home,
I saw you young, heard stories of you young as me,
your knickers stuffed with stolen cookies,
booty to share with kids you fought the day before.
The year you spent in bed, the several months
of dying you did live through.

I was proud and frightened.
You frightened me and made me proud
of what I might become, being your son.

One trip north
and our drive in country so much changed
you couldn't find for hours the place
you'd come for us to find.

II

And now it's merely light wind,
  the long light late in the day,
weeds giving way before you,
  I in your wake in the fields,
seed fastening to my pantlegs, your legs
thrashing free of burrs and the thorns and branches
I was trapped by, you against the sun, you tall
as trees, you graceful with your earned strength moving freely.

Then, in a stand of trees the colors of fire
the house you looked for: sagging roof, broken door
so jammed you had to force it down
with the whole forest looking on
and I looking on.

Inside, cobwebs everywhere. Antique windows
made the light antique as I heard you dressing upstairs
and your mother downstairs calling you
and down the stairs you came.
The stairs collapsing now at the house's center.

III

Father, you could dance
and you learned to dance with pain.
They told you you could
never walk again.

Young and sure to die,
you lay and wept and wasted
in the bed of a closed room.
Then changed.
                    Changed
with such fierce strength
that curse became command.
You lived despite them all.
You rose, you walked, by god
you danced back into life.
I still cry when I hear
how, pale and agonized,
you made them watch you move.
You called it dance.
They did not understand.
You called it dance
and dancing it became.

IV

I will learn that from you.
Your eye's blue fire burned
with how I came to be.

How true you were, and strong,
and how suddenly gone.

I will redeem your blood.

I promise you your name.

FISHERMAN

A woman comes
to watch her lover pull nets from the sea.

His back bulges with ocean waves
contenting her a moment while his body,
black against the sun,
is swollen with such power
the slow dull sea around him trembles light.

She drops to her knees
and waits with sealight blowing in her hair
and with her skirt
she shades what she has brought.

Noon.

He sees her, shrugs the stone-gleam of his shoulder
and drags the living weight up onto land,
each wave trying to drag it back.

He joins her in dry grass beyond the sand.

Wine from a bottle tall and cool
in its wrapping of wet rags, a loaf,
a wedge of cheese, an apple and a knife.

While sunlight plays on dying fish
in thrashing brilliance
he chews and sees her eyes darken for him
and he is glad and laughs.

They are young
and neither seems to notice
the distant net
flashing,

the frantic sound of a thousand fingers snapping.

A pale gull slowly wheels a relic circle,
then is gone.

THE JELLYFISH

There isn't much a man can do
about a grounded jellyfish
except step over it, or prod
it with his walking stick, and if
he has no walking stick, his shoe.
My feet were bare, so I leaned
to watch the waves relax around
the shiny melted-looking heap.

The jellyfish didn't move,
but then, of course, jellyfishes
don't. They navigate at best
like bottles: When the tide shifts
they bob and drift away. But who
has ever seen a living creature
with a note inside?
                    I found
an iridescent fish, uneaten
and twitching still, inside the gluey
drying bowel. I saw it jerk,
expand its gills, then quiver, arrested
loosely, loosely and forever.
It shone with pink and green, blue
and yellow, flashed profoundly silver
in each spasm. I knew it was dead
already, and only seemed to work
to free itself.
                As I tried to remove
the notion from my mind, the mound
it moved in, like a glassy brain,
was taken from me by a wave
that slid from the ocean without a sound.

POETRY AND REVOLUTION

We must not look for myths
to salvage
the mistakes of our lives.

We must salvage our lives.

ON THE POEMS

I don't really have much to say about the actual composition of my poems. I could hype it up with imaginary circumstances, but the fact is that when I'm doing my best writing the circumstances are the least exciting or interesting to any breed of observer. Something's happening but it's happening inside my head: if it can get out, it gets transferred through the poem itself. Even those times when my personal life is a mess (i.e., exciting?), real composition comes with a sensation like being in the eye of the storm, great calm and a sense of sanctuary. Sanctuary not from life but in it; not escape but what Hopkins called inscape.

"Fisherman" was written the same day I finished a long poem called "The Storm," in 1966, winter. "The House You Looked For" was done in first draft in '68, finished a year later. "Poetry and Revolution" in spring, '69. In a sense, the last two play off against each other. "House" looks to my father for an example, "Poetry and Revolution" says, as I read it, that myths—personal, historical, political, cultural, what have you—are inert forms, useless until vitalized by our own direct experience of them. (Knowing about them, understanding them, etc. etc., may "raise one's consciousness" but until consciousness is qualified and matured by action, by responsible involvement, mistakes and recoveries and reflection, it isn't wholly real, assimilated.)

Those two poems were written about the time when I really did begin changing my own life, quite blindly at first in series of very negative moves to get out of ruts I was comfortable in, then, slowly, I began to make a life that felt more like a life, my life, than it had before. A lot of travelling, a lot of new people, places, plenty of misgivings and regrets, and a gradual leveling off that feels better and better.

190

Gary Sange

Gary Sange was born in Oakland, California in 1938. He has B.A. and M.A. degrees from San Francisco State College where he studied under the poet James Schevill, and spent four years in the Iowa Writers' Workshop while also working on a Ph.D. in English. Currently he teaches contemporary poetry and conducts a workshop at Georgetown University in Washington, D.C. His poems have been in magazines like *The Quarterly Review of Literature, Field, New York Quarterly, Southern Poetry Review,* and *Shenandoah.*

LIGHTHOUSE KEEPER

I am rooted to a cliff
that can wreck what I warn.
In the sweeping light I spot
each time too late the mast

of a slowly vanishing
schooner half under
the beach—winded, split
by a cargo of fathoming sand.

For years I've been the only
survivor. My light is run now
by remote control.
I oil machinery
and wait to repair.

A dark hub in an oval room
I feel turned
by the spoke of light.
I am tired of being alert,
tired of keeping my eye out
for something irregular on the waves.

No more. It is late.
I must complete my dream
of schooners going down.

TRUCKDRIVER

After miles of the same oasis up ahead,
he never gets there before the sun goes down.

Now in a lit high cube of glass,
he drags an orange girder through the dark.

Horizons spin beneath his tires
and turn under the sky;

exits flag him down and disappear.
He will glance from the Interstate's aim

to check his wristwatch still curving time
toward seasons in his youth when he first drove alone

to clank chains through the purple snows
of Minnesota

or watch in Arizona the land turn orange
under the rusting sun.

Now fields side against him;
powerlines spark in the hot night.

Faces he'll never forget smack
against the windshield and keep him awake.

Tireshreds and the identity of small
dead animals keep him awake.

In the porkwood walls of the squat café,
the frycook raises a bad face.

She flattens with her spatula the burger on the grill;
walking stirs the batter of her flesh.

He will look the other way
and spend what's left of the night

on that bench over there
to watch the dawn come over the diesel sky

of Terre Haute like an oilslick or spilt cream.
Then follow out the turnpike to the detour sun.

SEPARATION

When I declared
our separation,
you made enough coffee
for me to stay up forever.

It has been late now
for hours; I stare
into the steaming dark I sip
and still cannot exhaust your urn.

I try to miss you—
to find a yearning
that will last. Instead
I rehearse your last instructions:

The cacti
on the windowsill
will need water
in three more days.

I await their thirst.

DRIVE IN MOVIE

Lifesize in a car,
I watch tall faces
outdoors on a screen.

Across the way,
two people
—floundering
above a dashboard—
go down under their own weight.

I've come here
to be out of place.
One when everyone's two,

I'm the reason why locks click;
I'm anybody's guess.

The sun in the movie
goes down after dark
and a moon comes up over
the screen.
It's time now: the end.
Doris and Cary kiss;
couples rise; backs arch—
rearview mirrors fill with lips.

As gravel is scurried,
and cars—throwing light
at one another—pass by,
I wait to fall behind.

A hundred warm speakers hang
speechless from their poles.

ON "DRIVE IN MOVIE"

I know that a poet's license should expire when he explicates his own poetry. I know as well that poems are supposed to stand on their own; I hope mine do. However, I want to risk the expiration of my license by attempting here to account for, perhaps to explicate, certain preoccupations that appear in my poem, "Drive In Movie," and that recur in several other poems that follow it. I need to do this because I am a largely unconscious writer while the speakers in several of my poems are very self-conscious. They have more authority than I do and a greater knowledge of what they want than I could ever presume to have. I am not being cute or coy when I say I never want to have to meet these speakers in person. Hopefully it's enough that I have gotten them out of my mind. I think I have created them to keep them at bay, to be free of having to become any one of them. Yet even as I write these words, I'm aware of that creeping, shrewd, ironic speaker emerging in my voice—sure I want it both ways: to be open with and to lurk behind myself at the same time.

I once had a diary that I overheard whispering in my dreams. I once had a real, imaginary friend that my mother had to hold one hand out for when we were crossing the street and he had his own place setting at our table. But he wouldn't eat and he always went to bed before I did. His name was Janra and he was often threatening to be seen.

Be all this what it may, the speaker in "Drive In Movie" says, "I've come here/to be out of place." His sense of alienation is not illusory but has outskirts and a vicinity as immediate as any place he might call home. His sense of purpose, perhaps mission, is so deliberate it sounds almost perverse. Among a crowd of bystanders, he has set out to be the bystander with the least presence. At this Drive In Movie, every individual is so cut off from every other that the idea of there being a center of focus, a screen with "tall faces," is a travesty of the prevailing alienation. For the speaker to be "lifesize" is a conspicuous distortion of the surreal scale that controls proportions at the Drive In Movie. In the world of this poem, "lifesize" is not large enough to be visible. Paradoxically, the capacity to vanish is a measure of preeminence. The people across the way become more interesting to us and the speaker when they disappear. It would seem that their absence from our sight is an inverse measure of their progress toward intimacy. And the speaker and consequently ourselves are vicarious voyeurs with nothing naked to go on. We are no more familiar with the lovers across the way than they are with one another or, for that matter, than they are with the movie. For their "intimacy" is raised and lowered; they are the passive recipients of inspirations that put them out of sight; they have come to a public place to witness intimacy, emulate love, in cars that enforce their closeness with locks that click against intrusions from anyone who might be so lonely as to want what they have.

The Drive In Movie is a place of cosmic as well as personal disjointment, a place of mechanical optical illusions and fortuitous timing—just as the moon seems to rise on cue, so the couples watching the film rise on cue from the actors within it.

Within the context of the Drive In Movie, the speaker is a recognized stranger among unacknowledged strangers; his solitude cuddles in among their attempts at intimacy. He insinuates himself as an outcome of a drama they must overlook. He must dramatize the magnitude of vacuums people can't fill and, thereby, affirm the reality of his own. He wants to go beyond "the end" and "waits to fall behind" because he needs independently to extend suspense beyond the designated experience of the film. The emptied Drive In Movie is the ultimate theater for his self-consciousness. His voice is the interior monologue the "speakers" resume when the audience goes home.

Several of the speakers or figures in my poems strain to stay up later than anyone ever has before; one seeks to reclaim an abandoned depot with his solitude; one would design his own anonymity by joining a circus pulling out on the outskirts of town; another must go to sleep in order to complete his dream of schooners going down; and still another will follow out a turnpike to the detour sun. Above all they vanish or live by "threatening to be last seen."

Dennis Schmitz

Dennis Schmitz was born in Dubuque, Iowa in 1937. He was educated at Loras College and the University of Chicago, and currently teaches at Sacramento State College in California. His published books are: *We Weep For Our Strangeness* (1969), *Double Exposures* (1971), and *Monstrous Pictures of Whales* (1972).

where I lived the river
  lay like a blue wrist
between the bluffs & the islands
were tiny unctions of green. where
  every morning the horses outside
my house woke the sun & their breath
was like wet foliage
  in the cool air. but in my house
my bedroom poised
  between shadow & light & the light
was flawed by angles of glass
till night disappeared in a moment
  of wonder. the farm fed
on the full hillsides & sheets
of grain seemed to fall
  almost to the river's shore.
but from my window the farm
  was less real: the river & at noon
the fish I could almost hear fading
in its cool depths distracted
  the boy of twelve. my brother
beside me
  slept. he was oldest & duty
has deliberate solitude: even my sisters
kept their dolls
  quietly.

the second son: his father
is silent. whose hands are fouled
  with the birth of a new foal & the brother
fixes the blanket
over the mare's belly. the blood! & the younger
  boy thinks the flesh
a burden & at fault
  for its own pain. the others
lift the foal & pull
the small genital till it flexes
with full life.

I stood in the barn
born second of God's beasts
   & alone in the days of my making.

my grandfather's God
guided him to the river & the Holy
   Ghost, he said, hung
like a white hand over this hill. our farm
   was his & when he died
my father (his son) worked a stone
in the shape of a bird, wings
   upraised as if startled
by my grandfather's death.

my name came from the river
the Fox call "Father" &
   "Source" as if a man's semen
were the only cause & my mother's fluid
   a mere aspiration. my mother
told of monsters who may
have died in the river-bed & she read
   that ice a mile high once
moved over their bones. at night
   the river with cold friction
pushes my slumbering flesh
   & my manhood moves
new
& in its own seed.

my father
   died, feeder of so many horses & so fine
an ear he had
he heard the birds with feathered weight
   drop between the green rows
of corn. a gothic
man knowing
no wisdom & in that field we
   no longer plant. the birds
forever float
   above his grave & the ground

gives
more each year.

that winter the farm
    dozed, its tillage deep
in snow. the river
backs a cruel spine against
    the bluffs & boyhood's
dim fish ride
up under the ice, Mother:
    your children. inside
the fire rubs
itself for warmth & the windows
go white with frost.

IF I COULD MEET GOD

if I could meet God
as an animal
my mouth filled with grass
I would not talk
for he knows the smell
of grass
& the great choking
one must have
who seeks to swallow
his world
when an animal dies
his choking is not laughter
he does not shuffle
like a man who forgets
his key
he knows there is no door
he walks inside himself
his belly full
his ears erect with certainty

THE RABBIT LEAVES

the rabbit leaves
a track
like two dry fingers
in the new snow
the new season! & I have put
my fingers
once to a dying rabbit's
guts
that wound like roads
between the bones
where the bung-hole opens
on the white fur
like an eye

ON "ECLOGUES"

"Eclogues" is the first section in a three-part sequence of poems. The river (Mississippi) is central to the sequence. This part traces the narrator's origins. It shows his participation in the life the river gives, which seems to him unending. The last stanza emphasizes the irony, the anxiety, implied by the framework of reminiscence.

I wanted to duplicate the tactile landscape: backwaters, ridges, the complex transitions of light and shape between open field and forest as the river shifts from channel to channel. I hoped, by playing enjambments against the patterns of alliteration and assonance, to show the movement of the river and re-inforce the parallel movement of the narrator's life.

There are a number of conventional archetypal patterns (the mythic mother, seasonal-bodily changes, the generations of humans identified with certain animals, etc.) the image of the river suggested. If they function as they should—coincidentally—they outline more boldly the real people of the poem, help them recognize one another.

Mary Shumway

Mary Shumway was born in 1926 and raised in Wisconsin Dells, Wisconsin. She has a B.A. from the University of Chicago, an M.A. from San Francisco State College, and a Ph.D. from the University of Denver. She has taught in a number of colleges and universities as well as being a clerk in an Indian Trading Post, an insurance underwriter, a newspaper reporter, and a statistician. A Robert Frost Fellow at Bread Loaf in 1969, and a winner of an award from the Academy of American Poets, her poems have been published in *Chicago Review, The Beloit Poetry Journal, Denver Quarterly, Commonweal, Motive,* and *Prairie Schooner.* A collection of her poetry, *Song of the Archer,* was published in 1964 by Henry Regnery Publishing Company.

RIVER ROAD

After the spring floods, after
the easy down when the river follows
the rose, and marble-eyed, the carp
nest high in the birch, I hunt

the heron moorings of the river lice
where firs from their hutches nose
the quiet air, and reeds sniff after
blackbirds in the marsh. And cast

two shadows. One that wanders,
another roots where the millwheel
mosses, where harsh from velvet rise
the plop and hickett of the frogs.

The pads walk water when the earth
is rung, but never move. Floods
fall each spring and August follows,
scums this slough where now I stay,

where moorings fly, and suns cast
a curious shadow

BEFORE THE DARK IS DOWN

After the last long agate beach
we climbed the rise to watch stars
leap upwind in the ambient black

*turn once more
and say goodnight*

Shadows whistle up the Klamath,
and plankton, nursed on this last
sun's season, light a following tide

Tonight down Mendocino the Jeremiah
foghorns cast their nets of lamentations
on the coastal oaks. Tomorrow we return
and I should let you sleep

but turn
turn once more before the dark
is down
and say goodnight

This last land's summer's gone
and you close your eyes, indifferent
to the certain conflagration of the dawn.
Your fluent arms in sleep have altered
seasons in the following land; in tides
as these, time slips the mind

Only for the moment. Behind red
firs an urgent sun rides a rip of wind
and with the light, again, goodbye

before we go
before the dark is down
turn once more
and say goodnight

GOOSEBERRY WINE

Gooseberry wine of a twelfth moon
spilled down the land, tart winds
shook stars loose in my eyes.

A bouquet of fog fall-rooted in the river
crisped the woods and tightened the shore
for winter. Somewhere along the sand

a bush crackled leaving a fragrance
in the fill where a muskrat from a ledge
of ice drank current

and the high still night puddled
where the wine fell. From autumn lakes
I drew a brittle thing, minnows sculptured

from a bush where once the berries grew.
Now from this hand
the long applause of silence:

I lift to morning's light
the emptied
land.

PASSAGE

light rides the wings of heron
the river quickens on the boulder slides
and the August blood begins its first migration

a beaver leaving his fallen birch slips off
shore and disappears where roots of sun
grow fibrous in slow earth

I watch you walk away, your back to the snow
snaking down the highway. You remember only
the storms of apple blossoms in the land

spring's cottonwood blizzards and the hand
of summer on your cheek and I must go
though the slow smile begin with morning flocks

to warm the failing land. An alteration has begun.
I know winter by the fall of rimed hooves
wind whinnying from the cirrus fields

and I must go. This is a broken time. There will be
no frailing call, only the long empty answer
of hibernal sun

ON "GOOSEBERRY WINE"

One December night driving south out of Stevens Point on the land bridge across the Plover I saw a muskrat drinking, it appeared, from the flowage, the only part of the river not yet frozen. The moist air hazed over the open water and the light of a full moon gave it the color of gooseberries. At the time I had no idea that wine was made of gooseberries, although I suppose I ought to have known it from my childhood memory of their taste, their tartness. In any case, the scene became a paradigm for the transformation of life into art: the process is the poem. By morning the world would be iced, still—a kind of suspended life, life caught in the eternal poise we sometimes call a painting, a sculpture, a piece of music, a poem. The paradox of art itself was there for me, the transformation both perpetuates and destroys. Life is time. Art is timeless. Eternal. Perpetual poise. Because I lived the land as a kid, natural imagery structures most of my poems, and that night I saw the Plover, the earth, as a glass from which I drank that wine. Lifting the emptied land, however, to the *morning light* seemed to preserve that confounding ambiguity integral to all art, a salute to the prevailing force, finally—an acknowledgement of the crucial temporality itself of life, the focal poem.

Charles Simic

Charles Simic has written four books of poetry: *What the Grass Says* (1967), *Somewhere Among Us a Stone is Taking Notes,* and *Dismantling the Silence* (1971), and *White* (1972). Born in Chicago in 1938, he is a graduate of New York University, and presently is teaching at California State College in Hayward. His translation of Vasko Popa's *The Little Box* was published in 1970.

BUTCHER SHOP

Sometimes walking late at night
I stop before a closed butcher shop.
There is a single light in the store
Like the light in which the convict digs his tunnel.

An apron hangs on the hook:
The blood on it smeared into a map
Of the great continents of blood,
The great rivers and oceans of blood.

There are knives that glitter like altars
In a dark church
Where they bring the cripple and the imbecile
To be healed.

There is a wooden slab where bones are broken,
Scraped clean:—a river dried to its bed
Where I am fed,
Where deep in the night I hear a voice.

POEM

Every morning I forget how it is.
I watch the smoke mount
In great strides above the city.
I belong to no one.

Then, I remember my shoes,
How I have to put them on,
How bending over to tie them up
I will look into the earth.

THE WIND

Touching me, you touch
The country that has exiled you.

BONES

My roof is covered with pigeon bones.
I do not disturb them. I leave them
Where they are, warm
In their beds of feathers.

At night I think I hear the bones,
The little skulls cracking against the tin,
For the wind is blowing softly, so softly,
As if a cricket were singing inside a tulip . . .

What is joy to me is grief to others.
I feel grief all around my house
Like a ring of beasts circling a camp fire
Before dawn.

TAPESTRY

It hangs from heaven to earth.
There are trees in it, cities, rivers,
small pigs and moons. In one corner
snow is falling over a charging cavalry,
in another women are planting rice.

You can also see:
a chicken carried off by a fox,
a naked couple on their wedding night,
a column of smoke,
an evil-eyed woman spitting into a pail of milk.

What is behind it?
—Space, plenty of empty space.

And who is talking now?
—A man asleep under a hat.

And when he wakes up?
—He'll go into the barbershop.
They'll shave his beard, nose, ears and hair
To look like everyone else.

Where it says snow
read teeth-marks of a virgin
Where it says knife read
you passed through my bones
like a police-whistle
Where it says table read horse
Where it says horse read my migrant's bundle
Apples are to remain apples
Each time a hat appears
think of Isaac Newton
reading the Old Testament
Remove all periods
They are scars made by words
I couldn't bring myself to say
Put a finger over each sunrise
it will blind you otherwise
That damn ant is still stirring
Will there be time left to list
all errors to replace
all hands guns owls plates
all cigars ponds woods and reach
that beer-bottle my greatest mistake
the word I allowed to be written
when I should have shouted
her name

ON "BUTCHER SHOP"

Every space is an interior space. Even the starry-sky on a cold November night over the Pacific is a room. More precisely a childhood room, for these spaces have ancient origins. For me the act of seeing consists of allowing the world to enter my first room.

Then there are walks. I love to stroll through a big city at night. These closed barbershops, drugstores, shoestores, pawn-shops, remind me of booths at a fair. There are no rifles or targets to fire at, but I still aim, I have no choice but to aim.

What first moves me are the images of solitude. That, however, is not enough to begin a poem. There is something else. It is time, or rather, the complete absence of it. Intimacy of emptiness. Here is an interior, here is a small universe completely indifferent to my own existence. I feel like an intruder and so I am afraid. I have walked too far.

I am sure that many such moments were required. The poem is not the testimony of one particular occasion, although it was probably written very quickly. My purpose was to capture the depth and complexity of the experience. I let it dictate its own terms. I had no other plans. To theorize about an interior as I am doing now is only possible after the poem is made. This is an activity which cannot hope to capture the essential.

To return now to what I said at the beginning. What we have here is a mirror. One gets a brief glimpse of oneself. One catches oneself existing, looking on an alien reality. The poem consists of retracing the steps, of making the journey to that point of clarity where "I am fed," where the *other* notices my presence.

David Smith

David Smith was born in 1942 in Portsmouth, Virginia. He has a B.A. from the University of Virginia and an M.A. from Southern Illinois University. He has been a high school football coach, bartender, and teacher. After spending four years in the United States Air Force, he is presently in graduate school working on a Ph.D. His first collection of poems, *Mean Rufus Throw-Down*, was published by Basilisk Press in 1972.

MEAN RUFUS THROW-DOWN

He waits perpetually crouched, teeth,
tongue, raw knuckles, tattooed muscles
bunched under his hide like clouds,
taking and taking and taking until
the right moment tears his eyes open,
his arm, like a lover's curse, snakes
swiftly out to second eating the silky
air of the proudest runner, ending the game.

DYING OFF EGG ISLAND BAR

—For Larry Lieberman

I hung like a man on trapeze, my arms stiffening
into spines, my feet feathering the water as the last
blood in my veins gives up its body heat for the cold
precision of swimming, my face buried in the womanish
tufts of seaweed.
          I can see the shadowy shapes of divers
as I turn, holding my flanks tinglingly rigid, a curious Angel-
fish or thick-lipped Gourami, to their groping hands.
What could I tell them that would save me? I have cried
all the sounds that will travel underwater, have coiled
against their warmth like guppies in the open palms
of miniature women.
          Still they dove and plunged like eels
throwing the searing hook until I was lost in the funnels
of sand they drew at their feet. I have watched them
discharge their bubbled breath day after day, sniffing
among the sea creatures for a trail I might have left
until bored, they wandered
          hoping to discover some shipwreck
full of bright coins which my family weeping in the dark
might accept in exchange for their efforts. But I followed
them in the murky depths, pressed myself on their thighs,
gave them my name, and spoke of my airless tumbling
like an unconscious child.

Who do you think you are, spiny man,
they said, drawing themselves back into rings of light
they spread from their hands. Do you think freewheeling
like that, driving yourself through ballets is enough
to convince us you are alive?

What could I say to such hammerheaded
bonefish? Help me? Take me back to the shimmery eclipse
of boats I could see overhead? Let me in the close glass
with which you cover your face? Give me everything you have
because I have nothing?

Touch me, I tried to say, just touch me.
I will ride on the string of your hand, I will rise
to your call, a loving porpoise, gibbering for my life
content to be the fool of the crowd forever. Such sounds
I made that their ears stopped with pain. But there were
no words sharp enough.

So I hung as they rose up and out
giving my family the empty shrug. I felt my eyes stuck
into parallel wedges and after a while the current swept
me into its course. On the morning of the first day
I lay in a bed of delicate moss, phosphorous burning
away the last of my flesh, and minnows fought over me.
I saw I was free at last and lazily considered how
I would use my blue infinity.

HOW ONE THING LEADS TO ANOTHER

Cusp

the little word
I have found
in a Nemerov
poem.

I let it
roll
over my tongue

like a glinting
ball of mercury;

cusp.

How it swells,
gleams   snaps,
hooks its horns
in an old cavity
I have forgotten
to fill

like a backward
glance at a woman
I once loved.

Cusp.

The little pain.

ON "DYING OFF EGG ISLAND BAR"

Egg Island Bar is a sand bar off the small fishing community in which I
live. The water is clear and about chest deep at high tide so that in
small ways it resembles a vast aquarium. How it got into a poem I was
writing (or how the poem settled there) is only one of the mysteries I can
hardly pretend to understand. I think writing this poem is roughly
analogous to determining how a beautiful fruit develops a bruised spot:
it rolled from point to point until it sat long enough for various forces to
gang up and produce some kind of coalesced thing. To talk about the
poem I went to my notebooks.

   With surprise I found seven clearly identifiable earlier versions and a
number of unfinished starts with similar elements. The earliest was a
three line, seven stanza piece in which the speaker was not the victim
but an observing diver. My notes show I was unable to get what I
wanted: the narrative experience of a drowning man who may not yet be
technically dead, that is, a man cognizant of rescue efforts and his own
impending death who can do nothing but drift like a weed. I wanted a
"factual" possibility, not a fancied vision, a man who, if reached in
time, might be brought to the surface and life.

I remembered I had difficulty with this through the winter of 1969 and then in the summer witnessed an event which began to draw the poem together like a drawstring. Shoving off from a dock to go fishing I saw an old man lifted ashore, dead of a heart attack. Because of the distance I could not see his face and only later did I learn he was an old fisherman I had known fairly well. He had often told me stories of his life on the water, always with a bitterness born of the machine age which had destroyed the water, the livelihood he enjoyed, and the camaraderie of the old village. And always he ended with the almost Viking hope that he would die on the water. After this I mused on what I knew of him, his habit of heavy drinking which often flipped him from his boat so he had to hang onto net stakes until picked up: he had not in 68 years learned to swim, his fierce sense of "family," his passionate love of circuses, his extensive knowledge of and respect for sea creatures, his growing hatred of dredge boats, cars, bridges, and all the paraphernalia of the modern age.

I worked on the poem with little success in the spring of 1970. In June I heard on the television news of a young man who drowned on a bar like our own, whose body eluded the professional US Navy divers for three days. I discovered the narrator wanted to tell his own story, was neither young nor old, and imagined or described his experience in terms of tumbling underwater much as circus acrobats floated in mid-air. Somehow he wanted and reached out for two worlds, the infinite ease of the sea and its freedom and also the discipline of membership in a compassionate, human community. It became clear that whatever the result now, there would be a winning and a losing from his point of view.

I had been thinking of the death as a noble, if final end. But my narrator saw dying as an important act of potential affirmation, if it had to come to that, which yet might be denied. Either way the experience of the not-quite-dead man resonated with certain cultural value statements, a decision would be made, and a position posited which began and ended with the old man whom I had respected and loved. Of course this is all hindsight. Just as the first line of each stanza is swung out to the right in some kind of pseudo effort to suggest a continual "possibility of the alternate," I made other decisions from a variety of directions. Why or how the poem got its shape I can't coldly say. Only that I liked what I found. I still do.

David Steingass

David Steingass writes:

> Born 12 July 1940 in Ohio where I grew up on small
> & real farm, loving it all and really learning things
> from the whole experience: concentration, patience,
> fatigue of frustration, wonder of color and pattern . . .
> none of which I've seen since in any sort of form-
> ative grouping.

A writer of fiction as well as poetry, Steingass's work has appeared widely in periodicals. His first book, *Body Compass*, was published in 1969 in the Pitt Poetry Series by the University of Pittsburgh Press.

MIDWEST U.F.O.

She tosses, one midnight so close
The melons perspire on their loam,
And pitches stark awake in silence,
For no reason. The clock's luminous
Fingers point to a sprattled *Reader's
Digest* on the bed table, the county
Paper, her son's last letter
From the seminary in Wichita.
She touches it, her hands so white
From milkhouse disinfectant, they look
Sandblasted. She feels there is little
Time, and throws on the print, feed bag
Robe that was so pretty new,
Hurries past the lumped husband
To an apple grove behind the house,
Where she has come before.

It is not lonely, she thinks, breaking off
A twig, but only that the pastor
Comes each third Thursday for dinner.
An Ozark flight ponders overhead
Toward Pueblo. She knows the schedules.
There is not a light to see at night
And not another house by day.
She has memorized the Grange calendar.

Never on an airplane, she faces
With a shudder, never left the state.
The twig snaps in her hand, the leaves
Twist and crush. It takes a plane
Four hours all the way across.
On tiptoe, breathing all she can hold,
Stretching three thousand miles,
Good gray strands of hair over her nose,
She pulls her hands down her face.
The twigs catch in her hair.

A light like Christmas bulbs
Flickers inches from her nose.

The wind rises, blowing her hair
Right, catching her robe, writhing.
She runs at last, as she has not run
Ever, and the light twinkles
In conversation, friendly, warm.

It is saying something she can hear
Almost, beyond the farm and darkness,
Beyond anything, beyond New York,
And only to herself. Perhaps to land
Another night and speak, to look
At her as human,
To hear her explanation first:
They know where things are friendly.

THE SEVEN-YEAR BODY CYCLE: TO MY CELLS REPLACING THEMSELVES FOR THE FOURTH TIME

Make no mistake. This is not
Done lightly, and for my pain
I assume earth will tremble
In good Renaissance fashion.
I would accept meteor
Craters or a pestilence:
Anything that leaves traces.

And since they are mine, I give
You my darkness, my stomach,
Heart and falling hair. Take it
All: my overweight, my five-
Day beard, the skin I have
Forgotten, the bones that can
Not be reset to forget.

Most of all, my attitudes.
Dilute them with piney oil
And pass them out in food lines,
During national alerts.

I retain only the glow
Along the cuticles, felt
Once or twice at night, a strange
Air blowing along the thigh.

WISCONSIN FARM AUCTION

"Minneapolis, Midwest,"
McDonell says inside the airport.
"Okay. Show me the Great Plains."

Snowballs drop everywhere.
Sound drifts behind barns, back through
Windup victrolas in the yard and gathers
Under brass bed frames picketing the lawn.
The auctioneer's assistant sidles to McDonell,
Stands where the mattress wants to be, plumbs
An imaginary pillow. "Bet many a hired girl
Spent time here," palming
A brass posthead.
Ruddy farmers stamp the snow, their denim jackets
Flap red and black squared lining
Over zippered sheepskin vests.
Surfer hair eggbeaten, McDonell
Raises his arms and puffs at the sky.

A wooden cash register. "McClaskey, Alliance, Ohio."
Enameled keys. Rings and works, once
The dust is brushed away. Potato drill:
He holds it sideways. "You got a crocodile,
Maybe alligator. Lookit his mouth. Clomp!"
He slides a cabbage grater's wooden box
Along its grooves. Snowflakes plop
On the steel blades. Bloodstained
Sheepskin coat for a quarter. He looks
Like a Dalton brother, gunslinger
In Acme boots.

Three pairs of stiff horse harness,
The collars like misshapen leather innertubes.
We nail "collar horns" to the wall
(Two pairs are steamed ash,
One steel with metal ball-tips).
Bridle temples are brass rosettes and a string
Of ivory rings, dangling from an inch
To three and a half in diameter.
Dozens of buckles and cinches, huge
And little tongs, fluttings and whorls
Heft like turtles or bricks.
We buff the green with silver polish.
Solid bronze. Some pure brass! McDonell strings two
Around his neck.
"Indians would kill for these."

Twenty-five bucks for a buffalo robe.
The fur curls three dark brown inches,
Incredible, coarse hoary stuff
So massive it looks artificial.
We throw it on the couch.
It defies the room, dwarfs everything.
Wants to rise up and thunder somewhere.
Lies dead weight around the shoulders when we wear it,
Pounding us breathless in moments.
Perches rigid in a corner chair. We watch it sit
Higher than human.

That night McDonell was cold.
He dragged the buffalo through the dark
Upstairs to his bed, and slept
Until noon.

ON "MIDWEST U.F.O."

I like this poem because it was my first (after "Winter Morning Remem-
bered") which contained elements of "real" poetry, I thought, and be-
cause I felt I had found some emotional statement about growing up in
the Middle West.

My father and I were caught in the Unidentified Flying Object craze. Sometime during the fifties I presented him with a small hand telescope and sky guide for Christmas, but in reality the telescope was to get closer to the flying saucers we knew frequented Ohio and other Midwest states. Some nights went until 3 a.m. from my bedroom window ledge. If a person looks through a telescope for more than an hour things begin to move. We saw everything from eye flecks to orbiting satellites, I suppose, but we never saw anything whirl or spiral into the cornfield. Still, I've never been able to forget the sense of impending adventure (a kind of fairy tale of American technology). It all had to happen sometime during the fifties, I think, to offset the malaise of that decade.

Later research confirmed my idea that an overwhelming number of UFO sightings occurred in the geographical Midwest. The poem began with this fact coupled to my remembrance of long telescopic nights. In the fall of 1968, perhaps 10 years after the actuality, I wrote the poem within sight of the Pacific. The first three stanzas have been much revised; nevertheless, they read substantially as they came from my pencil. I remember the excitement: first, I sat for a long time thinking of a detail that would begin the poem in an offhand, yet "loaded" way, and finally I remembered Midwest humidity and melon patches. For the next 35 minutes I held a handwriting race.

I was consistently aware of the discovery of detail and imagery *through* the writing, things I knew but not until their turns came in the poem (for instance, the "sandblasted" effect of her hands). I was happy about the sound and meaning of "ponder," the rhythmic quality of the "lighthouse" couplet a few lines lower in the second stanza, and the fact that boredom could make feasible memorizing a calendar. Similarly, in the third stanza, "Stretching three thousand miles," and in the last, "Beyond anything, beyond New York," are metaphorical discoveries made *in the process of writing* the poem.

This is the only feminine narration I've written; people seem to think the P.O.V. odd. I never realized this until the poem was well finished, and by that time it belonged to the wife. I can't say consciously why I picked her. I don't think Midwest wives are lonelier than husbands, though possibly they are. Perhaps the influence comes from some of Anderson's finely drawn WINESBURG, OHIO women.

Leon Stokesbury

Leon Stokesbury was born in Oklahoma City, Oklahoma in 1944. He has degrees from Lamar University in Beaumont, Texas, where he is presently teaching, and the University of Arkansas. His poems have appeared in *The New Yorker, Prairie Schooner, Carolina Quarterly, Shenandoah,* and the Borestone *Best Poems of 1972.* In 1971 he won an award from *Southern Poetry Review*'s National Collegiate Poetry Contest.

TO LAURA PHELAN: 1880–1906

Drunk I have been. And drunk I was that night
I lugged your stone across the other graves,
to set you up a hundred yards away.
Flowers I found, then. Drunk I have been.
And am, standing here with no moon to spill
on the letters of your name; my loud fingers
feeling them out. The stone is mossed over.
And why must I bring myself in the dark
to stand here among the sour grasses
that stain my white jeans? Drunk I have been.
See, the thick dew slides on the trees, wet weeds,
wetness smears the air; and a vague surf
of wildflowers pushes my feet, slipping
close to my legs. When the thought comes at last
that people fall apart, that the things we do
will not do. Ends. Then, we come to scenes
like this. This scene of you. You apart:
this is not you; and yet, this is where I stand
and close my eyes, and feel the ragged wind
blow red and maul my hair. In the night somewhere,
dandelions foam. This is not you. Drunk
I have been. Across this graveyard, that
is where you are. Yet I stand here. Would ask
things of your name. Would wish. Would not be told
of the stink in the skull, the eye's collapse.
Would be told something new, something unknown.—
A mosquito bites my hand. The only sound
is the rough wind. Drunk I have been,
here, at the loam's maw, before this stone
of yours, which is not you. Which is.

SUMMER IN FAIRBANKS

is like a dull dream. From time to time
the paper boy comes grinning with proof that
something has happened after all. Here

224   *Leon Stokesbury*

where the highways end. To go north
from here, you must be a bird or wealthy.
The prospectors have each been starved and strained
away down southward and to old folks homes.
Here is where the nights end too. Never
to sense the dark for days is strange, and not
so hot as one might think. It is strange
always to be able to see, and say:
that is there and that is there and that
is over there, always. Strange, not to tell
the end of days by any other way
than clocks, and meals; televisions turning off.
Different, for things to seem
to the eye like one day, that somehow
has slowed down to months, years, icebergs
of minutes so separated by an absence
from anything that ever came before,
that the anxious people find themselves
waiting for the swish on their lime lawns
of the dirty tennis shoes of
the grinning paper boy who brings them yesterday.

THE GRADUATE ASSISTANT
TELLS ABOUT HIS VISIT

Most people, of which I am
one, look upon themselves as
more-or-less experts about
being alone, loneliness,
large holes, etc., but
when, on a recent visit
to my great aunt, she told me
she had been writing quite long
letters for several years
to Lucky, her dead dog, I was
taken by surprise. Also
she said, "Now honey, I want
you to remember always

to keep your writing on the
highest level." I had sent
her a copy of a small
anthology in which I
did not cuss. I guess that was
what she meant. She seemed proud
of that; then, when I took her
out to eat at this Italian
place, the sky writers were
on the job, telling us to
go somewhere else. Well, she liked
the pepperoni pizza
OK, saying only, "There
really isn't too much here
for the price you have to pay."
I drank to that. Once again
outside, we saw the writing
on the sky had rotted all
away. Twilight was coming.
Already in the alleys
and clogging up the sewers
some fistulas of darkness
were floating around. And so
when I left her that evening
she kissed me on the cheek, then
took her handkerchief and wiped
the lipstick off. After which
miles fell between us. My aunt
is old, and she never went
to college. And so, I
think she knows, perhaps, nothing
or at the most very little
probably, of irony,
or of ambiguities,
or of anything that is
anything at all like that.

BACK BEHIND THE EYES

In this poem I am fast asleep in bed.
Over my head, there floats
a large and white oval bubble, in which
can be seen, not a log being sawed
by a saw, but instead, two people
familiar to me. They are turning to me
now and, yes, I have often seen them before.
It is a bare scene, frayed and vague
near the sides; but there is definitely
a door towards the back. And also towards the back
is a bed in which a small boy lies asleep.
The bubble over his head contains
a tiny chain saw that whines softly and whirrs.
Both parents say bitter things and wave
their arms vigorously. The upper lip
of each curls back revealing the obscene
pinkness of moist gums. And occasionally,
the mother cries and menstruates. Lightly,
lightly. Odors of shrimp. They take turns
exiting out the door in the back. While one
is gone, the other walks to the bed, picks up
the child, and always whispers in its ear.
The boy, wearing only underwear, and with
a birthmark on his thigh, listens to each parent
then sobs and sobs. This scene is repeated
perhaps twenty times. Sometimes the father
carries a bag of golf clubs with him
as he goes. Usually not. For many nights now
all this has recurred. It is, I suppose, a habit
to be quickly wakened from. And I will be.
I know that soon I will rise from this poem
and sit up in bed, looking over the side
as always, at the tops of my empty shoes,
two dark mouths opened, rightly, in horror
at what they are being asked to sustain.

You're probably wondering
what I'm doing with this
2-by-4 said a stable boy,
and when I came to with
dried blood in my ear
I knew that I had
missed the joke again.
It happens all the time:
that was no refried banana
that was my wife. That
means something? Meant nothing
to me while they grinned
their asses off. You go
straight to hell I said;
but I can't go through
life this way, always outside
watching the baker
plopping pastries into
sacks for other kids,
that's no good, I know
that for sure, but what
can I do, what can I
use for a ladder, what
to carry me up into
the loft, away from these
stinking horses?

ON "TO LAURA PHELAN: 1880–1906"

It seemed the right thing to do at the time. And we were really drunk.
So we took the tombstone, which must have weighed about 250 pounds,
and set it up in Jim Whitehead's front yard. This was about one in the
morning. Well, about nine in the morning Jim called me, explaining
that it was Mother's Day and his wife had not taken the joke in the
spirit that we had intended it and would we please come and get the
tombstone out of his yard and take it somewhere else, he didn't care
where. So we carted it back to the graveyard to put it back where it had

been for over sixty years. But we couldn't find the grave. It was an old graveyard, filled up years ago. Weeds had grown around most of the graves so you couldn't see some of the stones until you were right up on them. Not really feeling much inclination to hunt for the gravesite, we just set the stone in a vacant spot and I picked up some plastic flowers from one of the graves nearby and dropped them down in front of Laura's new place and we went on home.

That much is true. But a year or so later, late one night the idea of a return visit to the tombstone occurred to me. I didn't go. But I did begin to work out this poem about what might have happened if I had gone back. The thing that interested me about Laura was the fact that she had become her headstone. As far as anyone alive was concerned, all that remained of her was that rock with her name on it. As far as anyone alive is concerned, all that's left of Sir Thomas Wyatt are some poems with his name on them. "To Laura Phelan" is the result: a poem working through stream-of-consciousness and refrain and ending in what I think is my final statement these days on the big time themes of life and death and art. Many of what seem to me to be my best poems have begun, like this one, with some actual autobiographical fact that I have been able to twist and refocus until it became the poem and reality I wanted.

Some have asked about the refrain phrase, "Drunk I have been," and why it is inverted. My only answer is that it feels right and better than "I have been drunk," at least to me. The phrase allows me to make several moves that I otherwise might not have been able to make in such a small space. The refrain concludes one line of thought, enabling me to get on to the next one without interrupting the language flow. Sometimes it answers a question. Sometimes it clarifies my reactions to the scene.

The poem is written in a decasyllabic line, mostly. I enjoy writing my first drafts in a syllabic line. This allows me a freedom in form as I compose them. If I want the poem to move quickly it may have only seven syllables to the line with a great deal of enjambment. If it deals with a more serious theme, like "To Laura Phelan," the line tends to be a little longer. Later, I go back and improve the enjambments and whatever else needs improving. The poem is no longer strictly syllabic, but it is a better poem. Whatever it takes to get there.

Mark Strand

A native of Summerside, Prince Edward Island, Canada, Mark Strand was born in 1934. He was educated at Antioch College and Yale University, where he now teaches. His poems have appeared frequently in *The New Yorker*, and *The New York Review of Books*, and he is the author of three books of poems, *Sleeping With One Eye Open* (1964), *Reasons for Moving* (1968), and *Darker* (1970), and the editor of *The Contemporary American Poets*.

ELEGY FOR MY FATHER

(Robert Strand 1908–68)

1. The Empty Body

The hands were yours, the arms were yours,
But you were not there.
The eyes were yours, but they were closed and would not open.
The distant sun was there.
The moon poised on the hill's white shoulder was there.
The wind on Bedford Basin was there.
The pale green light of winter was there.
Your mouth was there,
But you were not there.
When somebody spoke, there was no answer.
Clouds in the blind air came down
And buried the buildings along the water,
And the water was silent.
The gulls stared.
The years, the hours, that would not find you
Turned in the wrists of others.
There was no pain. It had gone.
There were no secrets. There was nothing to say.
The shade scattered its ashes.
The body was yours, but you were not there.
The air shivered against its skin.
The dark leaned into its eyes.
But you were not there.

2. Answers

Why did you travel?
Because the house was cold.
Why did you travel?
Because it is what I have always done between sunset and sunrise.
What did you wear?
I wore a blue suit, a white shirt, yellow tie, and yellow socks.
What did you wear?
I wore nothing. A scarf of pain kept me warm.

Who did you sleep with?
I slept with a different woman each night.
Who did you sleep with?
I slept alone. I have always slept alone.
Why did you lie to me?
I always thought I told the truth.
Why did you lie to me?
Because the truth lies like nothing else and I love the truth.
Why are you going?
Because nothing means much to me anymore.
Why are you going?
I don't know. I have never known.
How long shall I wait for you?
Do not wait for me. I am tired and I want to lie down.
Are you tired and do you want to lie down?
Yes, I am tired and I want to lie down.

3. Your Dying

Nothing could stop you.
Not the best day. Not the quiet. Not the ocean rocking.
You went on with your dying.
Not the trees
Under which you walked, not the trees that shaded you.
Not the doctor
Who warned you, the white-haired young doctor who saved you once.
You went on with your dying.
Nothing could stop you. Not your son. Not your daughter
Who fed you and made you into a child again.
Not your son who thought you would live forever.
Not the wind that shook your lapels.
Not the stillness that offered itself to your motion.
Not your shoes that grew heavier.
Not your eyes that refused to look ahead.
Nothing could stop you.
You sat in your room and stared at the city
And went on with your dying.
You went to work and let the cold enter your clothes.
You let blood seep into your socks.
Your face turned white.

Your voice cracked in two.
You leaned on your cane.
But nothing could stop you.
Not your friends who gave you advice.
Not your son. Not your daughter who watched you grow small.
Not fatigue that lived in your sighs.
Not your lungs that would fill with water.
Not your sleeves that carried the pain of your arms.
Nothing could stop you.
You went on with your dying.
When you played with children you went on with your dying.
When you sat down to eat,
When you woke up at night, wet with tears, your body sobbing,
You went on with your dying.
Nothing could stop you.
Not the past.
Not the future with its good weather.
Not the view from your window, the view of the graveyard.
Not the city. Not the terrible city with its wooden buildings.
Not defeat. Not success.
You did nothing but go on with your dying.
You put your watch to your ear.
You felt yourself slipping.
You lay on the bed.
You folded your arms over your chest and you dreamed of the world
   without you.
Of the space under the trees,
Of the space in your room,
Of the spaces that would now be empty of you,
And you went on with your dying.
Nothing could stop you.
Not your breathing. Not your life.
Not the life you wanted.
Not the life you had.
Nothing could stop you.

4. Your Shadow

You have your shadow.
The places where you were have given it back.

The hallways and bare lawns of the orphanage have given it back.

The Newsboys Home has given it back.

The streets of New York have given it back and so have the streets of
Montreal.

The rooms in Belém where lizards would snap at mosquitos have given
it back.

The dark streets of Manaus and the damp streets of Rio have given it
back.

Mexico City where you wanted to leave it has given it back.

And Halifax where the harbor would wash its hands of you has given it
back.

You have your shadow.

When you traveled the white wake of your going sent your shadow
below, but when you arrived it was there to greet you.
You had your shadow.

The doorways you entered lifted your shadow from you and when you
went out, gave it back. You had your shadow.

Even when you forgot your shadow, you found it again; it had been
with you.

Once in the country the shade of a tree covered your shadow and you
were not known.

Once in the country you thought your shadow had been cast by
somebody else. Your shadow said nothing.

Your clothes carried your shadow inside; when you took them off, it
spread like the dark of your past.

And your words that float like leaves in an air that is lost, in a place no
one knows, gave you back your shadow.

Your friends gave you back your shadow.

Your enemies gave you back your shadow. They said it was heavy and
would cover your grave.

Your wife took your shadow and said she would keep it; she died and you
found it beside you on the bed.

You hated the sun because in the morning it would take your shadow
and at night would give it back unused, untouched.

The night was good for it was your shadow and you were large
surrounding the moon.

Winter took your shadow which lay like a long cape on the snow and
gave it back with your breath.

When you died your shadow slept at the mouth of the furnace and ate
ashes for bread.

It rejoiced among ruins.
It watched while others slept.
It shone like crystal among the tombs.
It composed itself like air.
It wanted to be like snow on water.
It wanted to be nothing, but that was not possible.
It came to my house.
It sat on my shoulders.
Your shadow is yours. I told it so. I said it was yours.
I have carried it with me too long. I give it back.

5. Mourning

They mourn for you.
When you rise at midnight,
When you rise and the dew glitters on the stone of your cheeks.
They mourn for you.
They lead you back into the empty house.
They carry the chairs and tables inside.
They sit you down and teach you to breathe.
And your breath burns,
It burns the pine box and the ashes fall like sunlight.
They give you a book and tell you to read.
They listen and their eyes fill with tears.
The women stroke your fingers.
They comb the yellow back into your hair.
They shave the frost from your beard.
They knead your thighs.
They dress you in fine clothes.
They rub your hands to keep them warm.
They feed you. They offer you money.
They get on their knees and beg you not to die.
When you rise at midnight they mourn for you.
They close their eyes and whisper your name over and over.
But they cannot drag the buried light from your veins.
They cannot reach your dreams.
Old man, there is no way.
Rise and keep rising, it does no good.
They mourn for you the way they can.

6. The New Year

It is winter and the new year.
Nobody knows you.
Away from the stars, from the rain of light,
You lie under the weather of stones.
There is no thread to lead you back.
Your friends doze in the dark
Of pleasure and cannot remember.
Nobody knows you. You are the neighbor of nothing.
You do not see the rain falling and the man walking away,
The soiled wind blowing its ashes across the city.
You do not see the sun dragging the moon like an echo.
You do not see the bruised heart go up in flames,
The skulls of the innocent turn into smoke.
You do not see the scars of plenty, the eyes without light.
It is over. It is winter and the new year.
The meek are hauling their skins into heaven.
The hopeless are suffering the cold with those who have nothing to hide.
It is over and nobody knows you.
There is starlight drifting on the black water.
There are stones in the sea no one has seen.
There is a shore and people are waiting.
And nothing comes back.
Because it is over.
Because there is silence instead of a name.
Because it is winter and the new year.

THE PREDICTION

That night the moon drifted over the pond,
turning the water to milk, and under
the boughs of the trees, the blue trees,
a young woman walked, and for an instant

the future came to her:
rain falling on her husband's grave, rain falling
on the lawns of her children, her own mouth
filling with cold air, strangers moving into her house,

a man in her room writing a poem, the moon drifting into it,
a woman strolling under its trees, thinking of death,
thinking of him thinking of her, and the wind rising
and taking the moon and leaving the paper dark.

Dear David Evans:

I cannot write on either of the poems. If I said something—no matter
what it was—it would sound foolish the next day and the day after that
and so on. Besides, I have nothing to say. If this makes my inclusion in
your anthology out of the question, I am sorry, but I feel strongly about
being silent on the subject of my own poems.

Best,
Mark Strand

Dabney Stuart

Dabney Stuart was born in Richmond, Virginia in 1937. A member of Phi Beta Kappa at Davidson College, he later attended Harvard as a Woodrow Wilson Scholar. Among his literary awards are the Howard Willet Prize for a summer's work on poetry, the Dylan Thomas Award from the Poetry Society of America, and a grant from the National Foundation on the Arts and Humanities. He has taught at the College of William and Mary and Middlebury College, and currently is at Washington and Lee University in Lexington, Virginia, where he is also poetry editor for *Shenandoah*. Recently his poems have appeared in *The New Yorker, Poetry, The Kenyon Review, Poetry Northwest, The Quarterly Review of Literature*, and other periodicals. His two books of poems are *The Diving Bell* (1966), and *A Particular Place* (1969), both published by Alfred A. Knopf.

THE FISHERMAN

Alcemon, a pupil of Pythagoras, thought that men die because they cannot join their beginning and their end.

—W. B. Yeats

Thick water laps
The seawall's edge as the tide ebbs,
Leaving its stain
On the shelved, gray stone.
Out past the shallows where crabs
Eke trails nobody maps

My sinker nudges the ooze.
Above it two barbed hooks
Wave in the current like weeds.
On this end of the line I practice tricks
To convince some sucker fish he needs
To play this game of what we've got to lose.

All day on the stone wall
And nothing's worked. The same cheap shrimp
I started with slog beyond the shoals,
Going nowhere. Long past cramps
Numb to my nape, in the ebbing light
I'm caught. How does a hooked man fight?

The thick dark flows around me half asleep:
Sparrows peck dung in a green street.
Gulls, hung above a liner's stern like kites,
Scrounge garbage. Vultures, who know their rights,
Pluck out a dead man's eyes. A winding sheet
Unrolls a sailor's body, lets it drop.

I wake. Though bottom-blind, afraid
These waters might yield
A catch so rich and strange that I could wield
It no better than my dreams, I wait
For whatever spawn or breed
Will take my bait.

POWER FAILURE

for Dan Hoffman

Somewhere the lines were down
He imagined the current expiring
Into the loose wind
Thrilling the darkness

His legs carried him to a candle
Its light moved
Breathing the dry air

I'll check the fuses he said
To be sure
And descended the long flight
Into stone

Beneath seasons
He found it cold
Did not remember the moisture
Nor the brute drawings
Flickering on the walls

When his fingers responded
He dropped the candle

Went by touch

His fingers fitting their prints

He was without direction
Following a vein in the rock
Did not know
When he passed through the crevice
Too small for his breath

And discovered himself
Kissing his wrists in a morning
Stunned by his bones' brightness.

HUNTER, PREY

Downwind, he caught the scent
Coming from where he had been

Turning
He waited for it to approach him

It covered his tracks
Bearing his prime intent
Until it stood where he stood

He recognized the place

The wind lifted to a great height
Trembling the roots of an aspen

And the sun focused through him
As through a lens

A stone burned with the light

HIS THIRD DECADE

I

Ends in a house
Collapsing into itself

Whatever direction the wind takes
There is a wall to receive it

Caught inside
At the last moment

The moment where four winds meet
And the walls give in
To what is beyond them

He finds himself
Unsafe anywhere
But tries the basement stairs, going
Down.

II

Ends on another flight
Beginning in wreckage

Going down from the moment
Where four winds met
No more than another frame
House already drawing in
Toward the one small life

His life

Which had never been
More than one place at a time.

III

Ends at the one small place
He had from the beginning

The winds' focus
To which the walls had fallen

Himself

Descending now beneath the foundation
He finds room enough

Meets all his fathers
In the taproot of an oak

Moves upward again through them
Into the winds   his brothers

Remembering it

As the bole expands
He counts the rings of his self
Collects the years, like bark

Lives here, lives
Here, giving this wood his name

Calling it home.

ON "HUNTER, PREY"

The general intention of all the poems printed here is the same: to
make a pattern that speaks of, and is, the attempt to strip off what seem
to be trappings and return to sources that are extremely distant and ex-
tremely close. I love language but I distrust the way the mind, my mind,
freezes it; these poems wish to thaw the surface and descend.

Beyond that sense of general intention it is difficult for me to go, as
I think it is difficult for anyone to go. I was not articulate about even
the general intention until after the poems were both written and then
arranged resonantly with each other. Anything I would say about par-
ticular whats and hows in the making of "Hunter, Prey" would be after
the fact. I choose this poem, in fact, because, of the four, it gives me the
fewest illusions about how it happened. All commentary is a reading;
there is no truth in these matters; art is a game, criticism is a joke,
though relatively harmless to everyone except the critic.

As one reader, then, of one poem, I would say that "Hunter, Prey"
moves to its final figure in a way I wish to move myself. Its sense, and
use, of space—a place called *here* with its converging distances, above and
beyond and previous—its imagination of physical impossibilities, the
speaker's sensory acuteness and his awareness of game (in both senses)
talk each other toward discipline, intensity and a life such as the story of
Orpheus' shadows.

As with everything I read, each time I read this poem I write it. It is
not over in any way I understand, and can act as a talisman for my craft.

I am being devious only as I experience the making of poems to be
devious. Above all, the process will not yield its secrets. If there are
rules, and there are as one devises them, there is also a sense that as they
are made they are changed, and somehow assist in approach only, never
arrival. That is, as I make it, what this poem is about.

Dennis Trudell

Dennis Trudell, born in 1938 in Buffalo, New York, has degrees from Denison University and the University of Iowa. After teaching in colleges in Wisconsin, Hawaii, and Pennsylvania, he is now living in Buffalo and working on a novel. His work has been published in a number of magazines and anthologies, and he is the author of three collections: *The Guest* (1971), *The August* (1971), and *Transient Tic* (1971).

39, 572

(*November 1969*)

Thirty-nine thousand
five hundred and seventy-two
times, our way alone, the membrane
between the mind of Christ
and a landslide of lasers and fishhooks
has torn. Thirty-nine
thousand five hundred and seventy-
two pet kittens, goldfish,
have been impaled. The shortstops
keep sliding into second
and out of sight. A scream
nearly four hundred thousand fingers deep
arcs over Pago Pago
and approaches Davenport.

Thirty-nine thousand five
hundred and seventy-two liquid clear
egglike sacs have felt
the explosion of incisors
to no music. That many
fathers, our way alone,
have seen the yawn of chasms
through their pillows (Some do
not know they see).

The navel fuzz
from government issue t-shirts
of thirty-nine
thousand five hundred and seventy-two
young men would smash
plate glass—
"But they don't wear t-shirts . .
too hot." Some fifteen thousand
paper routes have suddenly disappeared.
The mothers search vainly through hampers
for something to wash.

Tassels have cringed and unraveled
from the rear-view mirrors
of a city of cars. An unknown number
of letters now en route
are post scripts.
Perhaps twenty
thousand younger brothers
are afraid of their new sport coats.
Give or take. The nailed man
feels the sting from yet another
bayonet below the nipples;
the nipples have turned to cinder
thirty-nine thousand
five hundred and seventy three
times. Our way alone.
Their way, fragments of
so many straw toys clot the air.
Their way: . .
I cannot see beyond
the mountain of eyelids.

"YOU GET THE GROCERIES, I'LL GUARD THE CRIB"

It's one of those storybook days.

The trees are touseled oafs,
their bluejeans away
on the clotheslines of the moon.

The birds are former divots,
some of them, the rest are words
the baker's wife sent along
as her husband danced off with the highwayman's daughter.

The waves are a philosopher's
internal liquids; all are taken into account.

The clouds. The clouds are not
pale harmonicas, stuffed beyond all recognition, they are

not flimsy potatoes; the clouds are the cheeks of your old aunt
when someone used to raise them
to change the diaper.

The boys playing in the lots
are reincarnated glasses of water
from the maharaja's banquet.

The wind is what inhabitants of Uranus believe.

(Sometimes I think the birds
are doorknobs who wished)

The bushes are bones of unwritten operas.
Ones that smell fragrant would have been badly performed.

The afternoon begins to descend; the mood is gone.

EPILOGUE

    I have just joined a raggedy line
    of refugees at dusk. It is raw weather;
    the day was a foul wet breath. Tonight
    may bring the first snow: if not, tomorrow.
    The land is flat—treeless, mud.

    These people are carrying things. Children, blankets.
    Saucepans, poultry, books. Some are crying,
    some are very old. None are fat. And one
    is falling. Most are silent in several languages.
    They have read no newspaper in months.
    They are waiting to cross a bridge.
    By dawn there will be fewer;
    by noon there will be more.

I was driving across the island
to teach creative writing to the bent
at the Hawaii state hospital: no I was
in a short room listening to my grandfather
tell of the nightly feud in the lounge
over which channel to watch: I was standing
at three A.M. in the open window
of a German youth hostel peeing at the lawn,
a toilet two flights away: I think I
nodded as he said again how the nuns
who ran the place (my grandfather
was not Catholic) were plotting against him, a knock
came and I was shaking the two and one-half fingers
of his ex-carpenter friend
dying across the hall, they talked of *Gunsmoke*
for eight o'clock but the women would want
Lawrence Welk: I was nearing the pass
to the windward side wondering if Janet Sing's eyes
would be clear that morning, I would read
them O. Henry, try not to flinch
if the dialogue read "nuts" or "crazy":
I was holding a stiff Attention
in front of a waspy sergeant, I would show them
college men could take it (I loved my country):
I couldn't believe it—instead of a soft pat
onto grass rang the sound of my stream
on a tin roof, every hosteller must be
hearing (the frauleins upstairs—
how could I appear for breakfast?):
I was through the mountains ah the ocean:
I shaved him once, the stubs
fell like dry snow, the flesh was loose:
I was standing behind my suitcase
riding an escalator to an airplane:
I was walking in the rain after Kennedy was shot,
the first one: I was alone sometimes, sometimes
I had a friend, I was

young once, I was alive, I was
just sitting here tonight needing to touch
someone or make these scratches
on the silence.

ON "39,572"

There have been times when it has felt to me that I am unique, and in a
way that would make something fresh and true if I were to put words
onto paper. Often this occurs as a phrase—sometimes one word, less often
an image—and a tingle, a phrase and a tingle and something in me strain-
ing toward a surface to place my elbows upon and follow with a pencil
where they can lead. I usually know beforehand if the result is to be
what I will call a poem rather than a story by the amount of time and
kind of energy I am willing to risk: if I'm sitting up late with beer, or
have entered the relative neutrality of a snack bar or library, providing
an occasion, I am likely to wake up to or carry home a poem. If I sit
down to a whole morning and a plot in mind, perhaps some fiction. Al-
though the other has happened: short irregular-shaped entities brought
back from a block of hours that was supposed to make the bend of a story
or inch ahead the novel. But the groups of words only tentatively exist
at this point: whether I keep them or not is something I try not to
decide until after they have been typed and sat for awhile. I have dis-
carded scores of half-fish, dishonest windfalls, second-hand strums. Usu-
ally the ones I keep are more or less as they first occurred, though that's
no rule.

"39,572" began while reading the *Courier-Express* one morning while
drinking coffee at the Hotel Lafayette in Buffalo. As I was about to go
across the street to the public library and begin the day's elbowing at
the novel I was writing. Reading a short wire-service story of the U.S.
casualties in Vietnam to that date, I was held by the numbers. For the
first time (I'd tried before to write of the war, but always rejected what came
as shallow or imitative. I felt, and feel, that the absence of live poetry
about the experience shows that American poets are Americans, some-
what numb toward the details of violence despite what they would like
to feel)—for the first time the numbers seemed to separate slightly and I
had a peek into the reality they replace. Just a peek. It was enough to
allow me, several hours later, lying across our bed at home with a note-
pad, to begin the start-and-stop process and burrowing and selection—of
indulgence and caution, more indulgence than caution—which is the
writing of a poem.

I can't say anything about why certain choices were made over others. Once underway, the emerging hunk of language evolved its own laws of evolution; and the laws, if not (in this case) the final creature, were lost en route.

Afterward I am larger and less opaque. More easeful. A nice man.

One more thing. This is a poem about the horror of unnecessary pain and death, but rereading the poem does not make me feel horrible. If anything, I take something restful from it—something of the peace that may be what I am always aiming at when I write. For I am never able to forget, perhaps never wish to, that I am in the deliberate act of writing what may be a poem: which I will want to have published, hear good things about. At the end, whatever pain I've felt to say, may be the pride of having said it.

Alice Walker

Alice Walker was born in Eatonton, Georgia in 1944. She attended Spelman College, and received her B.A. from Sarah Lawrence College. She has worked in voter registration in Georgia, in welfare rights in New York City and has traveled widely and lived with families and groups in Kenya, Uganda, and the Soviet Union. She has been a writer in residence at Jackson State College and at Tougaloo College, and is currently teaching writing at Wellesley College and a course on black women writers at the University of Massachusetts. She is presently a Radcliffe Fellow, and her numerous awards include the Merrill Fellowship for writing, and a grant from the National Endowment for the Arts. Her published works include *Once* (1968), a collection of poems; *The Third Life of George Copeland* (1970), and *Revolutionary Petunias,* which will be published by Harcourt Brace Jovanovich in 1973. She is working on a book on *Langston Hughes* and a collection of short stories to be entitled *In Love & Trouble, Stories of Black Women.*

v

It is true—
I've always loved
the daring
                    ones
Like the black young
man
Who tried
to crash
All barriers
at once,
   wanted to
swim
At a white
beach (in Alabama)
Nude.

MORNINGS/OF AN IMPOSSIBLE LOVE

On the morning you woke beside me—already thinking of going away—the sun did not fill my window as it does most mornings. Instead there was cloud and threat of snow. How I wish it could always be this way—that on mornings he cannot come himself, the sun might send me you.

Watching you frown at your face in the mirror this morning I almost thought you disapproved of the little dark shadow standing behind you its arms around your waist. . . .

Two mornings ago you left my little house. Only two steps from my fingers & you were gone, swallowed down swiftly by my spiral stairs. . . .

Why do you wish to give me over to someone else? "Such and such young man you're sure to like" you say "for he is a fine, cheerful fellow, very sensitive" and one thing and another. Sometimes it is as if you'd never listened to my heartbeat, never heard my breathing in your ear, never seen my eyes when you say such things. . . .

This is what you told me once. Must I believe you? "We are really Easterners, you and I. The rising of the Sun brings with it our whole Philosophy."

THE OLD WARRIOR TERROR

Did you hear?
After everything
the Old Warrior Terror
died a natural death at home,
in bed.
Just reward
for having proclaimed abroad
that True Believers never
doubt;
True Revolutionaries never
smile.

ON "THE OLD WARRIOR TERROR"

I am for freedom beyond the freedom of the skin, and against whoever or whatever designs to limit The Person to less than he or she might be. Even limitation for one's own good (*especially* "for one's own good,") is suspect. When Revolutionaries become self-righteous enough to dictate when other people may smile, the Revolution dies prematurely, in Reaction. In the worst of times Person must still be Person. I am for people who defy and elude Judgment. I *liked* the irrepressible twinkle in Che Guevara's eye.

J. D. Whitney

J. D. Whitney has three books of poems, *Hello* (1965), *Tracks* (1969), and *The Nabisco Warehouse* (1971). Born in 1940 in California and raised there and in Detroit, Michigan, he attended the University of Michigan. Presently he lives in Wausau, Wisconsin, where he teaches at a branch of Wisconsin State University. His poems have appeared in *The Beloit Poetry Journal, Caterpillar, El Corno Emplumado, Epoch, Hearse, The Far Point, Elizabeth,* and other publications.

HERE

           he sd please
take it
            it
is heavy
heavy &
            I have
brought it
                all
the way here
here a
            muddled
happiness
for you
                always.
Whining
            she
whined yes I had
always meant
                        not
to be
here.
        He
gave it to her &
she
        taking it
in her
            2 hands
took it.

THE GIFT

When the tv has been turned off
and the news
            slowly sinks
into the dark throat of the screen
then it is time for all parents

to call their gentle
            musical children
into the livingroom
to sit at their feet
in a circle of wonder around them.
It will be quiet.
            The tension of
tongues must not be broken
as the parents undress
before the softly puzzled eyes
of their children
who will be held
            briefly
and for the last time
in that first clear moment of necessity.
First
      the father will
part their mother's hair
and make a swift incision
from the bridge of her nose
straight up
            back
over the head
            and down
to the nape of her neck
as
   taking the instrument
from his trembling hands
she parts
            his
hair.
And then the two will stand facing
hands on each
            other's heads
both
      grasping the flaps
of skin
and hair
and with a terrible pull down to the feet
the heaps of wet skin

```
                    slowly
folding into themselves
they will step out
                    red
as the low sun
sinking
          far beyond
stunned children
more pure
                than gratitude.
```

BEDTIME

```
          ceremony
Judy upstairs
counting with her
fingers in her ears
David in the
                dirty clothes
peeking thru a crotch
all 4 yrs
          hunch tight &
happy in his eyes &
me with no
new place to hide so
standing in the kitchen sink
face
       behind a dishtowel I can
see thru
          squeal
of being caught
                  hot
shiver in the dark downstairs
&
   one more round &
him to bed
& us to bed &
here we go again.
```

ON "HERE"

Hard to speak of one's own poem without wearing a stance, the poet playing dress-up, either way. Were I able to say what I was trying to do in a poem or how I went about accomplishing that intention, I'd call the poem in question aborted. Been sd before, & tho it sounds like a laziness, the poem that's born alive really does teach me its own what & how. Projective, yes.

But I can say how I respond to the poem; 5 minutes after the FACT of the poem's coming, I'm another reader.

The poem "Here" for instance. I like the rhythm as speech, the shifts of pace and weight as they move thru the short lines giving the situation made in the poem a desperate unurgency.

I like the flatness of the circumstances in the poem because I believe that each instance (&/or what happens in it) is an isolate somehow tied to another & another. For me, the flatness of the poem's language reinforces this sense that I am shown an unadorned instance in the lives of people who wd not have it so, but do. No metaphor at all: the reference to "heaviness" I hear to be quite literal, & that, for me, is exactly the terror of the poem.

I like the play of ambiguity & repetition & paradox, making the flatness pregnant.

& I like seeing the author getting away from his lyric thing. I'm glad to see him get other people into his poems, who are more interesting; glad to see his presence as ego in the poems yield to a concern for the dramatic & the narrative. An otherness here in which new people are born into their own otherness, & I take that to be more interesting than listening to a man articulate himself.

Al Young

Al Young was born in 1939 in Ocean Springs, Mississippi, grew up in the South and in Detroit, and was educated at the University of Michigan and the University of California at Berkeley. He has worked as a disk jockey, professional musician, lab assistant, yard clerk for the Southern Pacific Railroad, medical photographer, Spanish tutor, book reviewer, and actor. Presently he teaches in the Creative Writing Center at Stanford University. He is the author of a novel, *Snakes* (1970), and two books of poetry, *Dancing* (1969), and *The Song Turning Back on Itself* (1971).

SQUIRRELS

Squirrels are skittering
outside thru the trees
of my bedroom window,
laying it on the line
of my consciousness

Brown & black, furry &
scurrying, how can I not
help loving them like
an old bopster loves licks
laid down building up
so many beats to the moment?

Squirrels may be crazy
but they arent dullards
They like to play too
They cant be hustling nuts &
hoard all the time. Like
everybody else they love
a good chase now & again

Swishing thru branch leaves,
drumming on my diamond roof,
the shining young squirrels
are making & saving the day

GROUPIE

Cocaine and quiet beers
sweet candy and caramel
pass the time and dry the tears
on a street called buy and sell
                    —Laura Nyro

Evening isnt so much a playland as it is
a rumpus room, a place where harmony
isnt always complementary & where

spaces between palmtrees of the heart
arent always so spread out.

                      By 3 a.m.
there's love in her hose for the sailor
of saxophones or guitars & she'll try & take
the whole night into her skilled mouth
as tho that were the lover she really wanted
to rub against when all the time true love
inhabits her own fingernails & unshaven body.

You love her for the mental whore she is,
the clothed sun in Libra, the horny sister
who with her loose hair flying can get
no better attention for the time being

TRIBUTE

Yes brothers you invented jazz
& now I'm inventing myself
as lean & prone to deviance
as the brilliance of your
musical utterance, a wind
that sweeps again & again
thru my American window

What a life you sent me
running out into expecting
everyone to know at once
just what it was I was
talking or not talking about

The genius of our race
has far from run its course
& if the rhythms & melody
I lay down this long street
to paradise arent concrete

enough it can only be because
lately Ive grown used to taking
a cozier route than that of
my contemporary ancestors

Where you once walked or ran
or railroaded your way thru
I now fly, caressing the sturdy
air with balls of my feet
flapping my arms & zeroing

LONELINESS

The poet is the dreamer.
He dreams that the clock stops
& 100 angels wandering wild
drift into his chamber
where nothing has been settled

Should he get himself photographed
seated next to a mountain
like Chairman Mao
the real sun flashing golden
off his real eyes
like the light off stones
by oceans?

Give me your perfect hand
& touch me simply with a word,
one distillation of forever

Should he put his white tie on
with his black shirt
& pass himself off as a docile gangster
for the very last time?

The poet's dream is real
down to the last silver bullet

Should he slip again to Funland
in the city & throw dimes down holes
to watch hungry women flicker
one hair at a time
in kodacolor
from sad civilized boxes?

Should he practice magic
on politicians &
cause them to crack their necks
in a laughing fit?

The poet is the dreamer.
He dreams babies asleep in wombs
& counts the wasted sighs
lost in a flake of dusty semen
on a living thigh

Should he dream the end of an order
the abolition of the slave trade,
the restoration to life
of dead millions
filing daily past time clocks
dutifully gorging themselves
on self-hatred & emptiness?

Should he even dream
an end to loneliness,
the illusion that
we can do without
& have no need
of one another?

It is true that he needs you,
I need you,
I need your pain & magic,
I need you now more than ever
in every form & attitude—
gesturing with a rifle in your hand
starving in some earthly sector

or poised in heavenly meditation
listening to the wind
with the third ear
or staring into forever
with the ever-watchful third eye,
you are needed

The poet is the dreamer &
the poet is himself the dream
& in this dream
he shares your presence

Should he smash down walls
& expose the ignorance
beneath our lying noisiness?

No! No!
the gunshot he fires
up into the silent air
is to awaken

ON "SQUIRRELS"

"Squirrels" was written one friendly Fall morning after sitting on my porch railing in Addison Street, Palo Alto, California and watching them scamper up and down trees and telephone poles to the roof of my rented house. I'd been impressed with squirrels for years and wanted to get my feelings about them down onto paper. The time had never been right until that moment when I sat to write a very different poem—something about what it felt like to suddenly be 30-years old after years of painfully growing toward that magic age which seems to have some awful significance in our pitiable youth-oriented culture.

By the 4th or 5th line of the poem I'd intended to sweat out, it became as clear as light that what I really wanted to write was a quiet, admiring statement about all the beautiful squirrels whose lives and activities had graced my own. That's what I love about the process of writing: I'm forever setting out for one shore and reaching another. The lines poured out, slowly, spontaneously, in pretty much the order now comprising the present version. I dutifully took it down in longhand and dropped it into a drawer to allow a lot of time to pass before I looked at it again. This is my usual way of writing poems. When a few months had passed, I took the poem out to look at again and could see straightway that it still had meaning and that it was OK to sail it out into the world for others to share.

It took longer than a few months for me to realize how I had unknowingly—unconsciously in any event—tapped one of my inner life sources, music and musical lore, in composing this poem.

As a teenager I'd been profoundly impressed with the music of Tadd Dameron, a very creative although little-known composer-arranger-pianist whose original ideas had great imaginative impact upon such formidable modern jazzmen as Charlie Parker, Fats Navarro, Dizzy Gillespie, Miles Davis and Charles Mingus. Dameron, who's never been accorded the credit due him as an important American composer, wrote a tune called "The Squirrel," an up-tempo boppish figure set in a traditional 12-bar blues format. The melody, like that of most memorable jazz vehicles, is quite rhythmically seductive:

> *Weee dot-dot-dot-daaa-dot-DOT*
> *Weee dot-dot-dot-daaa-dot-DOT-DOT*
> *Weee dot-dot-dot-daaa-dot-DOT-DOT-DOT!*

In other words, the melody is constructed in such a way as to sonically suggest the image of actual squirrels scurrying about, adding *one*, now *two*, now *three* nuts, say, to some mutual hoard. So when I speak in the poem of loving them like an old bopster loving licks building up so many beats to the moment (or something like that), I was probably touching subconsciously upon my own obviously private interpretation of Dameron's tune and projecting what I'd heard into my personal vision of that morning's squirrels and what they were all about.

For what it's worth, the term squirrel, in 1940s and early 50s underground parlance, referred to a provident junkie who compellingly stashed a little away for those inevitable rainy days that lie eternally ahead.

I myself am a happiness addict who's always storing up excuses to be brazenly ecstatic.

My everyday trip is poetry.

Photo Credits

p. 1. James Applewhite. Photograph by Henry Applewhite. p. 10. Coleman Barks. Photograph by Ed Fortson. p. 16. Marvin Bell. Photograph by La Verne Harrell Clark. p. 23. Harold Bond. Photograph by Frederick Foltz. p. 28. Van K. Brock. Photograph by Malles. p. 35. Thomas Brush. p. 40. Raymond Carver. Photograph by Gary McNair. p. 46. Peter Cooley. p. 53. Sam Cornish. Photograph by Phyliss Ewen. p. 58. Tom Crawford. Photograph by Larry Rosengren. p. 63. Philip Dacey. p. 69. Stephen Dunn. Photograph by Howard Mohr. p. 75. David Allan Evans. Photograph by Noble Dallison. p. 81. Siv Cedering Fox. p. 86. Virginia Gilbert. p. 92. Robert Gillespie. p. 98. Elton Glaser. p. 103. Louise Glück. Photograph by Mike Annania p. 108. Albert Goldbarth. Photograph by Barbara Waters. p. 115. Michael S. Harper. p. 121. Phillip Hey. p. 127. Ron Ikan p. 131. Erica Jong. p. 138. R. P. Kingston. Photograph by Carolyn Cole. p. 143. Maxine Kumin. Photograph by Jed Fielding. p. 149. Greg Kuzma. p. 156. Larry Levis. Photograph by John Reed Forsman. p. 161. Thomas Lux. Photograph by Kathy Bodnar. p. 166. Morton Marcus. Photograph by John Carney. p. 173. William Matthews. p. 181. Tom McKeown. p. 185. William Pitt Root. Photograph by Rick Sterry. p. 191. Gary Sange. p. 197. Dennis Schmitz. p. 202. Mary Shumway. Photograph by Phillip Studio. p. 207. Charles Simic. p. 212. David Smith. p. 217. David Steingass. p. 223. Leon Stokesbury. p. 230. Mark Strand. Photograph by Douglas Kent Hall. p. 238. Dabney Stuart. Photograph by Robert Lockhart. p. 244. Dennis Trudell. p. 251. Alice Walker. Photograph by Olive Pierce. p. 254. J. D. Whitney. p. 259. Al Young. Photograph by Christa Fleischmann.